Guiding Light

The Word Alive in Our Hearts

CYCLE B

Homilies by Fr. Joe Robinson

Shepherds of Christ Publications
P.O. Box 627
Madison (China), Indiana 47250 USA

Toll free USA: (888) 211-3041
Tel: (812) 273-8405
Fax: (812) 273-3182
Email: info@sofc.org
http://www.sofc.org

ISBN: 978-1-934222-52-2

Second Printing: 2018

Dedicated to Pope Francis

In Honor of Our Beloved Priests

100th Anniversary of Fatima
October 13, 2017

My dear priests, hierarchy and members of the mystical body of Christ,

I give my heart to Jesus and Mary with you in love.

Fr. Carter our founder wrote two very important books *Response to God's Love* and *Response in Christ*.

The following thoughts are inspired by these two books.

God first loved us.

We receive a sharing in Divine Life in baptism – our knowing and loving capacity is elevated.

We are human creatures and yet we see God's loving self-communication to us with our concomitant response to Him in love.

Man rejected this self-communication of God in original sin.

God on His part communicates His own life through grace and man in return gives himself to God and his fellowman in loving service.

We can respond to this marvelous gift God gives to us as members of the mystical body of Christ – with Christ our head.

We can be witnesses of Christ alive in us both in the Church and in the world because the Father, Son and Holy Spirit dwell in a special way, in our graced, baptized soul.

God wants such intimacy with us.

I, Rita Robinson Ring, have learned a lot about the spiritual life from Our Lord in daily Mass and in spending at least one hour a day before the Blessed Sacrament where Jesus is truly present in His Divinity and humanity, no less present than when He walked the earth.

I have been guided by Fr. Carter our founder and had the gift of my brother, Fr. Joe Robinson at Mass, Sunday, week days, funerals etc. and other priests who have helped us on our journey in Shepherds of Christ.

Through the Priestly Newsletter of Fr. Carter we circulated 17,000,000 Newsletters to Priests and Hierarchy since 1994. This is Fr. Joe's 11th book. We sent out most years to about 38,000 priests and hierarchy. We have circulated about 400,000 of Fr. Joe's homily books over 10 years to priests and hierarchy.

What a gift these homilies of Fr. Joe's are as he teaches us about Responding to God's love, being Christ a-live in this world as a witness to Jesus and teaching us about the Bread of Life: the Word and the Eucharist.

We pray for the priests and have since 1994 in prayer chapters. Our prayers have been translated in 8 languages with the *Imprimatur*. We especially pray 8 days every month with Mass and the Holy Eucharist exposed most of the days for the priests, the Church and the world. We pray 24 hours every day and night in China before the exposed Eucharist for the priests and the Church.

Please pray with us, the prayers, Fr. Carter, our Founder, gave us in 1994 centered in Consecration to the Hearts of Jesus and Mary praying for the priests, the Church and the world. Life is in Jesus.

With love,
Rita Robinson Ring and all at Shepherds of Christ

We want Adoration Chapels
around the world –
The Mighty Medicine

Table of Contents
Cycle B – 2017 / 2018

Certificate of Marriage

I, the undersigned, do hereby certify, that on the 25 day of June A.D. 19 36 in the church of St. Boniface I joined in the

Holy Bonds of Matrimony

William M. Robinson and Alice Weber

according to the rites of the Holy Roman Catholic Church.

Witness: Henry J. Robinson
Marie Weber

Rev. John H. Schwartz
Pastor

Dedicated to William and Alice Robinson.

Our Mother and Father married on
June 25, 1936 in St. Boniface Church, Cincinnati.

1st Sunday of Advent
November 30, 2014

INTRODUCTION – (*Isaiah 63, 16b-17. 19b; 64, 2-7*) A true prophet has an ability to see and know God more profoundly than anyone else can. In our first reading taken from Isaiah, the prophet recognized that when the Babylonians invaded and destroyed Israel, it was a disaster that the leaders of God's people brought upon themselves for having ignored the guidance God had tried to give them. After 50 years of captivity, the Persians, who conquered the Babylonians, allowed the Jews to return to their homeland, Israel. The job of rebuilding what had been destroyed 50 years earlier was enormous. With this background, we hear the prophet lament how God's people are now suffering and, in the name of God's wayward people, the prophet prays for their heavenly Father to forgive them and help them. Just notice some of these beautiful expressions in the prayer: "Oh that you would rend the heavens (tear them open) and come down. Would that you might meet us doing right...Behold, you are angry, and we are sinful...our guilt carries us away...Yet, you are our father, we are the work of your hands."

HOMILY – (*Mark 13, 33-37*) A new Church Year begins today. There are no parties, no Champagne being uncorked, no funny hats or noise makers or staying up until midnight. As a matter of fact, it is quite the opposite. So we can be more open to Christ's coming, there are no flowers, the Gloria is not said or sung, the vestments are violet - a symbolic color for penance. Without any fanfare there is a change of gospels. We have been hearing from Matthew and suddenly today we heard from the gospel of Mark. The gospel of Matthew is laid aside until we take it up again two years from now.

It might be useful to say a couple of things about St. Mark since we will be hearing from his gospel for most of this coming year. Mark is the shortest of the three gospels and also the oldest. It was written most probably in Rome sometime between the years 64-67. Tradition describes Mark as the interpreter of Peter. That is, he wrote down whatever he remembered of Peter's proclamation of the good news about Jesus Christ. That's what the word gospel means: "good news." Mark was writing simply for the Christian community at Rome. About 10 or 20 years after Mark, Matthew and Luke wrote their gospels - also written for their own Christian communities. Matthew and Luke borrowed heavily from Mark in writing their gospels as well as including additional materials they had available to them. Today's gospel is unusually short, but its message is profound. Three times Jesus tells his followers (including us) to be watchful, to be awake, to be alert. He doesn't mean we need to stay up all night watching TV or something. He wants us to be awake, waiting for his coming.

His coming is threefold. First, he came in the past. The Son of God came to us and took on our human nature. We did nothing to earn this or to make this happen. It was God's own choice because of his great love and because of our great need for the blessings he could bring that he came to us. We profess this each week: "for us and for our salvation he came down from heaven and by the Holy Spirit he was incarnate of the Virgin Mary and became man." We celebrate this coming in a few weeks, but we must stay aware of what an awesome thing this is. As we focus on Christmas trees and gifts and cards and parties, we must also continue to be aware of God's infinite love, a love so great that he was moved to become human to teach us and forgive us and even suffer for us to bring us eternal life.

The second way he comes to us is in the present. He comes in his word, in the sacraments, in prayer and in the poor. We must be aware of these ways so we can recognize him and respond to him, listening to his word, letting ourselves be nourished by the sacraments, taking time to pray, helping those who come our way who have real needs.

The third way he comes to us is in the future. We do not know when that moment will arrive or in what manner it will arrive, but it will arrive for all of us. It could come as some great tragedy such as the attack on the Twin Towers on 911, or we could all leave this world (with or without warning) when our own personal time comes to leave. But we know for sure, 100 years from now, this world will be populated by a whole different group of people, and probably another billion more than we have right now. We will have moved on. We have to be ready and since we know not the day nor the hour, in order to be ready any time, we have to be ready all the time. Jesus' little parable in today's gospel tells us about a man traveling abroad and the uncertainty about the time of his return. That man is the Son of Man, Jesus, who told his apostles at the last supper: "I am going to go and get a place ready for you, then I will come back to take you with me so that where I am you also may be." When he comes knocking on our door may we be ready, may we greet him as a friend and not as a stranger. May we be watching and alert for his coming. Amen.

Feast of the Immaculate Conception
December 8, 2014

HOMILY – (*Genesis 3,9-15.20; Ephesians 1,3-6.11-12;*

Luke 1,26-38) Today's feast of the Immaculate Conception begins with a story about our first parents. They had been blessed with every blessing God could give them. That is what the Garden of Eden represents. Along with all these blessings, God gave them a Commandment not to eat the fruit of a certain tree and if they did, they would die. The devil showed up in the form of a serpent. The devil informed them that God gave them this command because God knew they would be just as great as God if they ate the fruit. So, our first parents decided that what God gave them was not good enough. They wanted to be as powerful as God. They didn't like God telling them what they could or couldn't do. They didn't want to have to obey God or depend on God. They wanted to be equal to God. So they ate the fruit they were not supposed to eat. Right away they knew they had done wrong. They began to feel shame and guilt. Then they began to put the blame on someone else for what they had done. Since there wasn't anyone else around whom they could blame, Adam blamed his wife and his wife blamed the devil. God told them they had been warned and now they and their children were going to lose many of the great blessings he had given them. They would also struggle with the tempter all their lives (talking to the serpent God said: "From now on you and the woman will be enemies, and your offspring and her offspring will be enemies...") Yet in the end, God spoke a word of hope; i.e., the tempter will cause some harm to the children of Adam and Eve (God told the tempter: "you will strike at his heel") but, God said, he (the offspring of Adam and Eve) will eventually overcome the forces of evil for "he will crush the head" of the serpent. We who are offspring of Adam and Eve continue to struggle against the evil one, and often we give in to the evil one, just as Adam and Eve did.

For many years God worked to prepare a way for evil to be defeated. He decided his Son would crush the head of the ancient serpent and destroy the power of the evil one. His Son would come to us in human form. When God was ready to send his Son, he decided that the mother of his Son would be totally free from any of the rebellion against God that somehow we inherited from our first parents. So God created Mary, free from sin, full of grace, for she would be the mother of God's Son. This is what the Immaculate Conception means. It is the feast we are celebrating. Mary, from the very first moment of her life, was free from sin. But it wasn't just for a short time that Mary was without sin. Mary lived her whole life, always ready to say "yes" to God in anything that God might ask of her. This was implied in the greeting the angel Gabriel used when he came to Mary. The angel said "Hail, full of grace!" Mary was very perplexed, but then Gabriel told her what God wanted her to do, "you will bear a son, and you shall name him Jesus. He will be great and will be called Son of the Most High..." Gabriel waited for her answer and, of course, like everything else in her life, her answer was "yes." "I am the servant of the Lord." Actually the word she used was "slave." She belonged to God and she would serve him in any manner he wished.

St. Paul sums up this beautiful feast in his letter to the Ephesians: "Blessed be the God and Father of our Lord Jesus Christ, who has blessed us in Christ with every spiritual blessing in the heavens, as he chose us in him, before the foundation of the world, to be holy and without blemish before him." God is blessed for having blessed us with every spiritual blessing so that we might be holy. The same gift of holiness that God gave Mary when he created her, he gives to us when we are baptized. I know we sometimes imitate Adam and Eve in deciding we don't like God telling us what to do, but let us pray that we might imitate Mary more, so we can enjoy God's spiritual blessings in heaven, forever. Amen.

2nd Sunday of Advent
December 7, 2014

INTRODUCTION – (*Isaiah 40, 1-5.9-11; II Peter 3, 8-14; Mark 1, 1-8*) When the Jews were conquered by the Babylonians in 587 BC, the ones who were not killed were taken to Babylon as slaves 1,000 miles away from their homeland. In spite of their sins, God promised not to abandon them; he assured them, through the prophets, that he would restore them to their homes and their lands. Roughly fifty years later the Babylonians were conquered and destroyed by the Persians (people who lived in Iran). The king of Persia, Cyrus, immediately gave the Jews permission to return to their land. Today's reading from Isaiah begins a large 16-chapter section of Isaiah known as the "Book of Consolation." The prophet is instructed by God to bring this good news of liberation to God's people. The route by which the Lord would lead his people home is referred to as "the way of the Lord." The prophet proclaims that attention must be given to preparing that way. This is the important theme in today's liturgy. John the Baptist takes up this theme five centuries later when he calls the people of his own day to prepare for the coming of the Messiah, of the House of David. The liturgy uses today's Scriptures to call us to prepare not only for one day, Christmas, but also for the various ways in which Christ comes to us in our daily lives as well as for the day when Christ will call us into his eternal kingdom.

HOMILY – Mark is the shortest of the gospels. He begins his gospel by informing us that we are going to hear about the good news of Jesus Christ; he doesn't start with the story of Jesus' birth as Matthew and Luke do, nor does he take us back before time began as John does. He gets right to the point and tells us we need to prepare to hear the good news of the gospel so that our hearts are open to God's Word. It is through John the Baptist that Mark tells us to prepare.

So much of our life is spent in preparation for one thing or another. God and nature began to prepare us for life in this world from the moment of conception. As we grew, we were taught how to adequately prepare ourselves for various events. I remember getting ready for school the first day and getting ready for my first Communion. I remember in the third grade having to move from Northside to Price Hill and all that was involved in getting ready to move. There were preparations for going to Elder as I graduated from St. Lawrence, preparations for entering the seminary, which was the first time in my life I was ever away from home. Preparing for ordination involved nine years of study and especially lots of activity during the last year before ordination. I thought I was well prepared to work in a parish and teach school. Little did I know how little I knew when I started and how many more ways I would have to prepare myself for the ministry I felt called to. I remember preparing to go to Israel for three months with only one suitcase and a carry-on bag. It was a lot of anxiety trying to make sure I wasn't forgetting something. Then there are the many routine things that require preparation such as holidays, family gatherings, preaching a homily every week, etc.

You're probably saying I don't need to hear all that, but I'm sure you could resonate with me how making preparations for something is such a big part of anyone's life. Think what an embarrassment or even a disaster we run into when we are caught unprepared. I remember sweating bullets as I sat in front of my theology professor during an oral exam. I can't remember if I studied the wrong material or my mind just shut down, but the result was not pretty. The prophet says prepare, John the Baptist says prepare, our advent season says prepare. For 1400 years, the Church has been celebrating this period of preparation. We are about to celebrate the greatest event in the history of the world; the Son of God has taken on our own human nature in order to reveal his love to us, in order to heal us, to teach us, to free us from sin and shame and to share with us everlasting life. If that's not important enough to prepare for, what is?

How can we prepare? Perhaps we need to change some habits or attitudes that conflict with Jesus' teachings. Perhaps we could read the gospel for the day, picture it, think about it for several minutes. Sometimes we can experience the Lord speaking to us in a powerful way through his Word. Or we could say the rosary during the week, or come to morning Mass or Holy Hour on Wednesday morning or Friday afternoon, or do some spiritual reading. There is no limit to the hundreds of kind things we can do for another person. Sometimes our preparations are not a matter of doing something more, but of doing something less (such as watching TV) so that we can have some quiet time to be with God. There's no substitute for quiet time. The spiritual and emotional benefits of quiet time are abundant. Don't just prepare for Christmas, prepare for Christ. Amen.

3rd Sunday of Advent
December 14, 2014

INTRODUCTION – (*Isaiah 61, 1-2a. 10-11; 1 Thessalonians 5, 16-24; John 1, 6- 8. 19-28*) As the celebration of Christ's birth draws near, the mood of our liturgy becomes more joyful. It's still Advent though, so we're not yet singing Christmas carols at Mass. We are preparing and waiting and praying for God to help us open our minds and hearts to the great miracle of his birth. Isaiah, in today's first reading, sees the day when God's kingdom would bring peace and justice to those who suffer and he rejoices as he sees this coming to be. St. Luke tells us Jesus used these very words of the prophet Isaiah to describe what his ministry would be about as he gave his first homily. The responsorial psalm is almost always from the Book of Psalms, but today it is Mary's hymn of joy - called the Magnificat. It is a hymn of praise which she enthusiastically proclaimed when she visited her cousin Elizabeth after accepting God's invitation for her to be the mother of our Savior. St. Paul, in today's second reading, tells us to rejoice always. Linked with this he says that we should pray without ceasing. He also adds we should give thanks in all circumstances - all of which draws a connection between joy and prayer and gratitude.

HOMILY – Joy fills our hearts as we reflect on the mystery of our God and creator coming to us in human form. He comes to assure us of his infinite love for us and his desire to share that love with us for all eternity. When we come to today's gospel, however, the theme of joy seems to have disappeared. Although he leaped with joy in his mother's womb when Mary came to visit his mother, Elizabeth, what we know of John as an adult was that he was a very austere person and a fire and brimstone preacher. So I struggled a little to find any reference to joy in the gospel. I read that John preached we must make straight the way of the Lord. That is, of course, the way to true joy, to walk the road that God has shown to us. I would like to share with you another connection I think there is between John the Baptist and joy.

John knew who he was. Not knowing who we are and what our purpose is will prevent us from knowing joy. A lot of people thought maybe the Baptist was the Messiah. John clearly denied it. Nor was he the prophet promised to Moses; nor was he the prophet Elijah who the people were expecting to return from heaven – although he did fulfill their expectations by taking on the role and the life style of Elijah. John was just a voice crying out in the desert. He knew that about himself. He knew that he was not even worthy to untie the sandals of the One to come after him. It is questionable as to whether even slaves were required to do that for their master.

At Delphi in Greece, there once stood a temple to the Greek god Apollo. Only the ruins remain now. On one of the stones of that temple are carved the words "Know thyself." These two words have been interpreted in various ways throughout the centuries. They may have had a specific meaning for the Greek worshippers of Apollo, but I want to assure you they are an important message for those who want to grow spiritually. I have been listening to a series of lectures on St. Teresa's Interior Castle and this is one of the basic teachings of Teresa. We have to know ourselves if we are going to make progress in the spiritual life. We have to know our emotions, our dreams, our strengths and our weaknesses. Knowing ourselves honestly for who we are is true humility. When we make ourselves more than what we are, it is the sin of pride. However, when we are honestly aware of our good points, that is pride too, but it is a healthy form of pride. When we make ourselves less than what we are we are being dishonest and diminishing the gifts and abilities and wonder of the good things God has given us. A lot of people think humility is a matter of putting ourselves down. Low self-esteem is not humility.

Humility is honest self-esteem. And if we could see ourselves in the light of God's great love, we would be absolutely astounded how much we are loved.

A person who is not humble is not likely to be joyful because they are constantly demeaning themselves or they are constantly working to maintain an image that they are something other than they really are. The next question is "how do we attain this honest self-knowledge?" The answer is meditation. It is a journey toward self-knowledge. This self-knowledge will lead us to a more honest knowledge of God for God lives within us. "Do you not know that your body is a temple of the Holy Spirit which you have within you and that you are not your own?" (*I Cor. 6,19*)

Joy is the product of a life lived close to God. For joy, look into your own heart; if you find in your heart such sentiments as gratitude, thoughtfulness and kindness, love, a positive attitude, trust in God and awareness of God's love, then joy should soon be growing there. We can get too absorbed in material things at this time of the year and miss the joy that God wants us to have, joy that results from his blessings to us and our responding to him. If you want to reflect a bit more on joy, read today's second reading again. Paul sums it up very well. Amen.

4th Sunday of Advent
December 18, 2005

INTRODUCTION – (*2 Samuel 7,1–5, 8b–12, 14a,16; Luke 1, 26–38*) Our first reading goes back 1000 years before Christ to the time of king David in Jerusalem. You need to recall that when Moses led the people of Israel out of Egypt, almost 300 years before King David, God gave the people a special sign of his presence among them. That sign was the Arc of the Covenant. It looked something like this: a box in which were placed the 10 Commandments, a lid of gold and on the lid were two angels. The box was carried by two long poles because no one could touch the Arc. The two angels provided a throne for their invisible God, Yahweh. As Moses and the people moved through the desert and eventually into the promised land, the Arc was kept in a tent. Only designated people, and eventually only the high priest, could enter the tent and offer sacrifice to God. The Arc was still kept in a tent during the reign of King David. David had built himself a nice comfortable palace and he decided it was not right that the Arc, the special sign of God's presence with his people, was still kept in a tent. So he told his prophet, Nathan, that he would build a temple, a house for God. Nathan said "good idea," but God said "no." God said David had shed too much blood in his role as king, so he would have David's son, Solomon, build the temple after David died. But God was pleased with David's idea and blessed him. One of the special blessings David received was that David's line would never die out. One of his descendants would always be king over God's people. That's what is meant by the statement that God would "establish a house" for David. For about 400 years this proved to be true. Always the king of Judea was of the royal house of David. When the Babylonians conquered the Jews, that was the end of the kingship. But the Jews never forgot the promise God made to David and always waited for one who would come from David's family who would rescue God's people from their enemies and restore the kingdom to Israel. Since kings were anointed when they assumed power, the king they looked for was called the anointed one – the Hebrew word for "anointed one" is Messiah, in Greek the word is Christos. In the gospel of the annunciation, the angel Gabriel informs Mary that her son would be the fulfillment of these hopes. "The Lord God will give him the throne of David his father, and he will rule over the house of Jacob forever, and of his kingdom there will be no end."

HOMILY – The angel Gabriel announced the birth of a king: "the Lord God will give him the throne of David, his father, and he will rule over the house of Jacob forever, and of his kingdom there will be no end." I love the interesting way St. Luke begins to tell us about this. He first of all introduces Mary, but not in the usual way we introduce someone. We would have said, "I would like you to meet Mary. She's from Galilee and engaged to be married to Joseph." None of us would have dared to add to our introduction: "She's a virgin!" But it's a very important thing St. Luke wants us to know and he tells us she's a virgin even before he tells us Mary's name. Why? Because Mary would conceive in a miraculous way, through the power of the Holy Spirit. That alone was spectacular, but that was only the beginning of the most unique and wonderful event this world would ever see. This king, who would be conceived by the power of the Holy Spirit, would be more than the ordinary, run of the mill king. This king, the messiah, the christos; that is, the anointed one, would be king over a kingdom that would never end. To top that, because he was conceived by God's own Spirit, he would be the "Son of God."

This is an awesome mystery that God took on our human flesh and became like us in every way except sin. There is a special theological term for it: the Incarnation. The God, who dwelt among his people housed in a tent for many generations, now comes to live with his people as one of us, taking on our own flesh and blood. Sometimes people like to say Jesus was a great prophet or a great teacher or a great humanitarian but that's all he was. The gospels tell us he is the Son of God. If he was less than that, there was nothing great about him because he was a crazy man, full of delusion and paranoia. There is no in-between position we can take on Jesus. [In today's bulletin is a copy of the Catholic Update that gives a beautiful explanation of today's gospel. I highly recommend it.]

How we live our faith depends on how firmly we believe in this wonderful event. If we truly believe God has come into our world and into our lives through Jesus, shouldn't we try to spend time with him, shouldn't we try to get to know him better and follow him as well as possible? If we are not ready to do that, could it be that our faith is little more than a lot of words?

One last thought. I would like you to notice the respect God showed Mary in the annunciation. God didn't just tell her she would be the mother of such an awesome person. God asked her if she would be and waited for her answer. We have here a cue for how the Son of God can come to us more fully. We have here a cue for how Christmas can fully fill our hearts. We have here a cue for how to enjoy the blessings of his kingdom that will have no end. God's Son wants to live in each of us. As God did with Mary, God waits for each of us to answer him as to whether he is welcome. Are we able to say as Mary did: "I am the servant of the Lord. I will do whatever you want of me, Oh God."

Christmas
December 25, 2014

HOMILY – Last Friday I visited the 8th grade in our

school. We talked about many things, mostly Christmas, of course. I started off with a few jokes, like: What did Adam say on the day before Christmas? "It's Christmas, Eve!" (some liked it!)

Here's another: a child writes in response to a letter from Santa: "Dear Santa, Sorry for what I did in the past, and thank you for the Christmas letter – I love it. But what I really want for Christmas is $53 billion dollars." (Who said children don't know the value of money?)

One more. A man wrapped his Christmas presents in early November and when he had finished he realized he had used the wrong wrapping paper. The paper he used had Happy Birthday written on it. Rather than waste the paper, he wrote Jesus on it after the words Happy Birthday. Now that gets us to what we're here for.

One child wanted to know if December 25 was the actual day on which Jesus was born. My answer was no one knows exactly on what day Jesus was born, but we do know he lived. We need to celebrate Jesus' birth because this is one of the two greatest things that has happened in the history of our world (the other great thing is Jesus' resurrection). Even though we do not know the exact date, the event that happened has to be celebrated because if we don't celebrate it we will forget it. So, I tried to get them to think how great a thing Jesus' birth is. Our God, the creator of the universe, who is infinitely greater and more powerful than we can imagine, came to us and took on our human nature. He became like us in all things except sin. He had no sin because he always loved his heavenly father and didn't want to displease him. He got hungry and thirsty and tired. He needed to be fed when he was an infant. Perhaps he hurt himself playing games; maybe some other kids bullied him. He needed to learn how to walk and talk and to obey his parents. He had to learn how to pray and to go to Synagogue on the Sabbath. He was God even when he was a little baby. So I asked, now, isn't his coming to us and becoming human worth celebrating? One boy said, if that's so great why don't we celebrate it every day. I would like to think that he wasn't just thinking of getting presents or having a break from school every day when he asked that question but that he was impressed with the awesome mystery of God's coming to us. I was pleased to hear a couple of children answer that we celebrate this mystery every week when we come to Mass. I added with Mass daily it's possible to celebrate God's coming to us every day. But at least for one day, we put other things aside so we can focus more intently on this mystery and on the love of God that it shows us. We can't forget about the reason why Christ came to us because he loves us more than we can ever know. The great mystery of his coming and of his love is repeated again and again in the Mass.

We all know we live in a world where there is so much pain and sorrow, so much fighting and hatred and crime. Jesus came to tell us there is a better way. He showed us that way by showing us how he loved others, the poor, the stranger, those suffering and all of us sinners. Even in sickness and sadness, he would show us the way to hope and to an eternal dwelling where we will find joy with him forever. He told us the way we could find that eternal dwelling when he told us he is the way and the truth and the life.

In the sacrament of the Eucharist we are cele-brating, he comes to us again and shows us his love. Some people have problems believing in the Eucharist. If we can believe that God can come to us as human, why do people have difficulty believing God can come to us in the form of bread and wine. I often think that for the God of our universe to become human, he had to reach an infinite distance below his own greatness to do so. If he could do that, it was just a tiny little reach further for him to take on the form of bread and wine. And so we celebrate God's coming and his infinite love which we hope to be able to celebrate forever. Amen.

Feast of the Holy Family
December 29, 2002

INTRODUCTION – (*Sirach 3:2-6, 12-14; Col. 3:12-21; Luke 2:22-40*) The Christmas season will last for two more weeks. With Joseph taking Mary as his wife and with the birth of Jesus, a new family is founded and it is a holy one. Ben Sirach, who speaks to us in today's first reading, was a teacher in a Jerusalem school nearly 200 years before Christ was born. Sirach's instructions cover topics such as home life, business, courtship and marriage, travel and entertainment. He even offers proper etiquette for entertaining guests or how to behave when invited out. Today's passage deals with our relationship with our parents, the importance of respect and obedience when we're young, and patience and kindness when we get older and they are too. In our second reading, Paul is writing to counteract the heretical teachings of those who thought that salvation was reserved only for those who were members of certain secret cults. He tells us it's the ordinary virtues that everyone knows and anyone can practice that are important; such as compassion, kindness, humility, gentleness, patience, forgiveness and love. Notice the importance he places on religious virtues such as familiarity with the word of God, prayer, singing and thanksgiving. The Greek word for thanksgiving is Eucharistia. When husbands hear Paul talk about wives being submissive to their husbands, they sometimes do not hear what follows. There is a mutual giving and receiving that is needed in marriage.

HOMILY – When the Holy Family is put before us as a model for us to imitate, we feel that is impossible. They are so far beyond us in holiness that imitating them would be like any of us trying to play baseball like Mickey Mantle or Babe Ruth. Well, we may not be the perfect holy family, but we are a holy family if we are in God's grace. It's God's grace that makes us holy and if the members of our family stay in God's grace, we are a holy family. The only danger we face is becoming spiritually complacent and lazy. We never stay in the same place spiritually, we are either moving forward or backward, and unless we keep trying to grow in God's grace, we will end up slipping backward or even losing grace altogether. As we heard in the second reading, there are no secrets to living and growing in grace. It's just a matter of practicing the ordinary virtues we learned when we were young: kindness, humility, gentleness, patience, etc. Jesus summed them up in his famous answer about the greatest commandment: loving God as much as we can and loving our neighbor as ourselves. The neighbor that we most often neglect is the person or persons closest to us. We too often take each other for granted instead of making time for one another, helping each other, complimenting each other, thanking each other or being patient and forgiving of one another. Good relationships are made up of just so many little things.

I think at times we imagine the Holy Family lived a charmed life without problems or stress. Problems began even before Jesus was born when Joseph was about to break his engagement to Mary. Think for a moment where Jesus was born - not neat and clean like the little mangers we put up in our homes. He was born in a stable that probably was smelly and dirty, maybe damp and cold. In today's gospel we are told about their presenting Jesus in the Temple and offering the required sacrifice according to the law of the Lord. St. Luke is telling us they were poor, they offered the sacrifice of the poor. St. Luke, incidentally, is telling us they observed the laws of their Jewish faith and were obedient to God. We can't be holy and ignore the things God asks of us. As they went to the Temple, surely they were happy to be able to bring their child there. But then an old man came up to tell Mary her heart would some day be broken because of her child. What a chilling prophecy! Shortly after this St. Joseph is told by an angel to get out of the area, that the king is planning on killing their child. So they end up refugees in a foreign land for a few years. The only other event we know of during Jesus' youth was when he was 12 and he was lost in the Temple for three days. What a worry and concern that must have been. A holy family is not a family without problems or heart aches. It's how we deal with those problems that really matters. We must be faithful to God at all times and we must deal with each other with fairness, kindness, patience and love. May God's blessings be with you and your families today and throughout the coming year.

Mary, Mother of God
January 1, 2015

HOMILY – (*Numbers 6:22-27; Galatians 4:4-7; Luke 2: 16-21*) A man, driving a little too fast, was stopped by a police officer around 2:00 a.m. and he was asked where he was going at that time of night. He answered "I'm on my way to a lecture about the sins of alcohol abuse, as well as smoking and staying out late." "Really?" the officer replied. And who's giving that lecture at this time of night, your pastor?" "No, my wife," the man replied. (*The Joyful Noiseletter, Jan-Feb, 2015, pg 2*) That story applies to no one here, of course.

In the year 153 BC the Roman Senate chose January 1 as the start of a new year. It was the day on which the Roman councils took office. It is said the people celebrated with "boisterous joy, superstitious practices and gross orgies." The early Christians made January 1 a day of penance as a reaction against the excesses of the pagans.

Today is a holy day, however, not because it's the first day of a new year - although I couldn't think of a finer way to begin a new year than with special prayers, especially the Eucharist. We all know how desperate our world is in need of prayer. Today is a holy day for several reasons. It's just by coincidence that today is the octave of Christmas. The liturgy solemnly celebrates major feasts like Christmas and Easter for eight days, until the octave (the Latin word for eight), and the octave itself is always an important day. Also, today is the feast of Mary, the Mother of God, a title that was officially decreed in the Council of Ephesus in 431. This title gives special honor to Mary, but it also confirms what we believe about Jesus, that Jesus has two natures but is one person and Mary is his mother. This feast of Mary is the oldest feast of Mary in the Church's liturgical calendar. Many will remember this day as the feast of the circumcision of Jesus and the feast of the holy name of Jesus.

In our culture we get excited about new things. It may be a new car, a new i-phone, a new friend, a new fashion, a new movie, a new year, and with the word new attached to something, we tend to assume it's going to be better than the old. We tend not to think of new things or events that are unpleasant: like new taxes, new contagious disease, new aches and pains, new problems at work, new global confrontations, etc. So in our culture's enthusiasm for what is new, we focus on what wonderful things the new year can bring to us, which it may do. But, at this time we also need to reflect on the good things in our life that are part of our past that we bring with us into the new year, such things as our values, our relationships and especially our relationship with God.

Before I conclude, I have two more things to say. First of all someone sent me a quotation that was attributed to Mother Teresa. This quote may inspire us to make the most of the days ahead:

Life is an opportunity, benefit from it.

Life is beauty, admire it.

Life is a dream, realize it.

Life is a challenge, meet it.

Life is a duty, complete it.

Life is a game, play it.

Life is a promise, fulfill it.

Life is sorrow, overcome it.

Life is a song, sing it.

Life is a struggle, accept it.

Life is a tragedy, confront it.

Life is an adventure, dare it.

Life is luck, make it.

Life is life, fight for it.

My second point speaks of prayer. We need God's grace and help every day. If we didn't think we needed it, we wouldn't be here. And here, as in many other instances, we can look to Mary as an inspiration and a guide. St. Luke tells us, as he has told us in other places in his gospel, that Mary pondered in her heart the things God was doing in her life along with Joseph and Jesus. This pondering or reflection was prayer. There is only one way to get closer to God, which is what we all want, and that is we need to spend time reflecting on what God has done or is doing in us, taking time to think about God, spending time with him, and communicating with him, which we are about to do right now.

Feast of the Epiphany
January 4, 2015

INTRODUCTION – *(Isaiah 60:1-6; Ephesians 3:2-3,5-6; Matthew 2: 1-12)* Six centuries before Christ, Babylon was a great empire. The city of Babylon was located on the Euphrates, just about 100 miles south of modern day Baghdad. In 587 BC the Babylonians conquered Israel and marched the Jews who survived the conquest off to Babylon as slaves. The Jews have suffered in numerous ways throughout history. This exile was unquestionably one of the worst events they ever had to suffer. But God would not let them be annihilated. In spite of their unfaithfulness to God, they were still his chosen people. So fifty years later, the Persians (people living in modern day Iran) conquered the Babylonians, and they allowed the Jews to return home. The Jews found their city and their homeland still in shambles. Rebuilding was extremely difficult. Today's prophet, whom we hear in our first reading, tries to encourage the people and assure them Jerusalem would again be a great city. He sees Jerusalem becoming the center of spirituality and light for the whole world. The prophet foretells that people would come from everywhere to visit Jerusalem and to be nourished by the spiritual light and life radiating from it. St. Matthew sees this vision fulfilled in the birth of Jesus and the coming of the magi. Through Jesus, the message of God's love and salvation will radiate to all the world.

HOMILY – We all love to hear the story of the magi and to sing the familiar Christmas hymns that remind us of the story. When we hear about the magi, we can't help wondering who they were, whether they ever came into contact with Jesus later on, and why the other gospel writers didn't mention them. That must have been a big deal when they visited Jesus and Mary; why is it only Matthew tells us about it? For lack of more information with a few more details, and for lack of any reference to it in other New Testament literature, many scholars question whether this is a real historical event. From what I have been reading, I am convinced it really happened. Here's why: Every part of the story is historically probable. For example, 1) there was at that time, even among the Romans, the expectation that there would arise a semi-divine hero-ruler. The Roman author Virgil writes about such expectations. The emperor Caesar Augustus was viewed by many as this hero-ruler who brought peace throughout the empire. Nero too was a candidate for this divine status. 2) Astrologers and magi as a professional class are frequently mentioned in the literature of the times. Even though astrology was forbidden in the Old Testament, Judaism was deeply affected by the phenomenon, especially during the couple of centuries right before Christ. 3) In the Book of Numbers, the fourth book of the Bible, there quoted a prophecy by a pagan prophet named Balaam that goes back about 1200 years before Christ. Balaam (also called a magi in later writings) predicted that "a star shall come forth out of Jacob, and a scepter shall arise out of Israel." (Jacob and Israel are the same person). Thus it would have been expected by the

Jewish people that the birth of an important person, such as a king or a great leader, would be marked by some stellar occurrence. Historically, there is nothing in the least improbable about the magi traveling from Babylon to any location in the Middle East. Magi, because of their respected standing, would find a welcome anywhere, from royal courts to market places. The image of Herod in the gospel as paranoid and shamelessly cruel, killing all the newborn males in Bethlehem, is a historically accurate image of the kind of man he was. I personally see no reason to doubt the historicity of Matthew's story about the magi and I find arguments against its historicity as unconvincing.

I want to mention four points that are important for us to take away from the account of the magi. This event connects Jesus with Moses and thus pictures Jesus as a new leader of God's people. How does he make a connection with Moses you might ask? Remember how the pharaoh at the time of Moses ordered all newborn males to be killed for fear that the Israelites would eventually be able to overpower the Egyptians if the Israelites had enough men to fight. Many infants were killed under pharaoh, but Moses was saved from death and was pre-ordained by God to lead God's people to the Promised Land. Jesus too was saved from death by the flight of the Holy Family into Egypt, thus getting away from Herod, and he came to us in order to lead us to the Promised Land of heaven.

Another thing we can see in the story is that Matthew gives us a hint about Jesus' future suffering and death in that people were out to kill Jesus from the time he came into our world. The forces of evil could not wait to get their hands on him. The magi would have been gentiles and so Matthew is revealing to us the universality of the gospel; all people are invited to come to know him and worship him so he can lead them to eternal salvation. The invitation for all people to find Christ's light is repeated in other places in Matthew's gospel, especially at the end Right before his ascension, Jesus tells his apostles to "go out and make disciples of all nations baptizing them in the name of the Father and of the Son and of the Holy Spirit."

Finally, I think Matthew is telling all of us how to approach Jesus. We are to continue to search for him until we have found him and to pay him homage as the magi did. We are not to treat Jesus with indifference like the Jews, who had answers as to how he could be found, but were not interested enough to go to him.

We come to him today bringing our gifts, our time, our treasure, our love, our devotion. We know through faith, the Scriptures and the sacraments we have found him, and yet knowing we are still on a journey to get to know him better and to love him more, and we still have some distance to travel. That's why we're here today. Amen.

Baptism of the Lord
January 11, 2015

HOMILY – *(Isaiah 42:1-4,6-7; Acts 10:34-38; Mark 1: 7-11)* I wonder how many were surprised to see the Christmas decorations still up in Church. Well, liturgically we are still in the Christmas/Epiphany season. But it all ends this weekend. So, enjoy the flowers and the crib which you won't see again until next year around this time.

Let me say a word about the meaning of Epiphany, so you can see how the feast of Jesus' baptism fits into the theme of Epiphany. The word epiphany means an appearance, a revelation or a manifestation of something, especially something glorious or wonderful. We celebrated Epiphany last Sunday by hearing how the magi, who represented the Gentile world, found the Christ child. Today's feast is also part of Epiphany, in that, at Jesus' baptism, God reveals Jesus as his beloved Son.

We could actually stretch the theme of Epiphany to almost everything in the gospels because whatever Jesus did, he was revealing himself as God's Son - whether it was changing water into wine, casting out demons, forgiving sins, walking on water, calming a storm, feeding a multitude with a few loaves of bread, teaching God's law, healing the sick or raising the dead. John the Baptist said, "One mightier than I is coming after me." Thinking of all these things Jesus did tells us just how mighty Jesus is.

We rightly wonder why Jesus asked John the Baptist to baptize him. Jesus was so far superior to John (or for that matter, to anyone who ever lived). John acknowledged this in saying he wasn't worthy to untie Jesus' sandals. So why did Jesus ask for John's baptism, especially since John's baptism was a baptism of repentance? Jesus had no sins; he did not need to repent. I have managed to come up three possible answers as to why Jesus was baptized by John. It is possible that Jesus was baptized for all three of these reasons combined. First of all, Jesus' baptism demonstrated his solidarity with us in his human nature. In other words, just as we are, he was fully human in every way possible with the exception of sin. Another reason for Jesus' baptism by John suggests that Jesus was showing his support for the work of John the Baptist and perhaps also sharing in that work as he began his ministry. It is likely from what St. John's gospel tells us (*Jn. 3,22*) that Jesus started off as one of the disciples of the Baptist and so his baptism by John would have officially incorporated him into the ministry of John. A third possible reason for Jesus' baptism could be that God the Father directly inspired Jesus to be baptized so that God could express his delight in his Son: "you are" or "this is my beloved Son in whom I have taken delight."

As we know, John's baptism was not the sacrament of baptism which all of us have received. John said, "I have baptized you with water; he will baptize you with the Holy Spirit." John's baptism symbolized a spiritual cleansing and purification; the sacrament of baptism really produces a cleansing from all sin and it grants us the gift of God's grace and life.

I think it is good to occasionally reflect on the theme of baptism because it is the sacrament through which our sharing in Christ's life begins. One wise teacher said if you don't celebrate an event, you forget it. We always celebrate our birthdays – we don't forget that day. But I would bet only a handful of people here, if that many, know the day of their baptism – yet that was the day on which we were reborn as God's children. That was the day we could legitimately say to God: "Our Father..." That was the day that set a direction for our lives, to follow Christ's way. That was the day that gave us the hope to be able to enjoy eternal life with God. One of the special reasons for the Eucharist is to feed God's life in us. Just as we need to eat to keep alive, so the life of God in us needs to be nourished, and what better nourishment could it receive than to listen to God's Word and receive Christ's body and blood.

John the Baptist said Jesus would baptize with the Holy Spirit. May that Spirit, given to us at our baptism, continue to move us in the right direction until we enter into the fullness of eternal life in God's kingdom. Amen

2nd Sunday in Ordinary Time
January 15, 2006

HOMILY – (*I Samuel 3,3b-10.19; John 1,35-42*) Once while I was at another parish I went to visit a lady in the hospital. She was the mother of a large number of children (more than ten), several of them still in grade school. In our visit she disclosed to me that she thought she had a vocation to be a nun. It was both humorous and sad, sad that she was so seriously detached from real life and humorous because with all those children underfoot, I could see why she wanted to get away from it all. My point is that not every time we think we're getting a call from God is it really God calling us. Often when he really does call us, his call is not so easy to discern, or if we discern where it's coming from, we're not so quick to follow. For example, Moses was in no hurry to take on the job God was asking him to do, even though the message came with unmistakable clarity. Samuel, on the other hand, kept hearing God call, but didn't know it was God. It was his mentor, the high priest, Eli, who helped him know God's voice. When I felt God calling me to be a priest, I was excited about the idea until I reached puberty. Then I was hoping the idea would go away, but God kept calling like he did with Samuel. The call to the apostles seems to have taken place over the course of time, as they found themselves attracted by Jesus' powerful personality. We see in today's gospel that God's call does not always come out of the heavens but from another human being. The call to Andrew and an unnamed apostle (probably John) came from John the Baptist. Peter's call started with Andrew. It took a while after meeting Jesus before they gave up their lucrative business in order to be Jesus' disciple or as that word means, Jesus' student.

When God calls, we seldom know what we are getting ourselves into if we follow that call. Samuel didn't know that he would become a leader for God's people, that he would be a prophet and priest, that he would lead the Israelites into battle, and that he would raise up and depose kings. Mary, the mother of Jesus, didn't know what she was in for when she said "yes" to God. Nor did the apostles know that they would have to give up more than their fishing business, and that following Jesus would cost them their lives. Mother Teresa felt called to be a nun and started her vocation in the classroom. After almost 20 years of teaching she received what she described as a "call within the call" when she felt called to serve the poorest of the poor and start a new religious order. Martin Luther King could not have had any idea when he was in the seminary and getting "C's" in public speaking that he would be threatened daily, that he would be imprisoned for standing up for justice, that he would be facing angry crowds with equanimity and prayer for his persecutors, that he would one day be leading 200,000 people to the nation's capital to dramatize that all of America's citizens are endowed with certain unalienable rights, among which are life, liberty and the pursuit of happiness. Nor did he know that an assassin's bullet would end his life at age 39. If I had known when I entered the seminary some of the difficulties I would have to deal with as a priest, I would have said, "God, I can't do that. Find someone else." I'm glad I didn't know, I'm glad God was with me during hard times, and I'm glad I followed his call.

God's call sometimes disrupts our comfortable lives. But if God wants us he'll keep calling, like he did Samuel, as long as there's a chance we might respond.

Sometimes we need help in knowing what God's saying, sometimes we need to be pointed in the right direction, sometimes we need confirmation from others. For example, when I went to the seminary, the rector and staff didn't assume that I really had a calling. We had to go through nine years of schooling and a lot of scrutiny before ordination. When the lady in the hospital with all the kids told me she felt called to be a nun, I couldn't support her. Instead I reminded her that her real vocation was to take care of her children. I think it's extremely important to notice that Samuel was already in God's presence at the place where the Arc of the Covenant was being kept, and it was in the quiet of the night he heard the Lord. Almost every time I have heard the Lord speaking to me, it was when I was praying, reading the Scriptures or meditating.

Our environment calls to us from so many directions: TV, radio, e-mail, cell phones, beepers, billboards, etc., etc. A lot of times God gets put on hold so we can listen to a call from somewhere else. If we want to hear the Lord, we have to put all other voices on hold so God can get through. The only way we can do that is to set time aside. I have a phrase I use for myself all the time regarding prayer: "if you don't schedule it in, you schedule it out." We have to make time for the Lord if we're really going to hear him, and if we don't, we won't. Amen.

3rd Sunday in Ordinary Time
January 22, 2006

INTRODUCTION – (*Jonah 3,1-5.10; Mark 1,14-20*) Whenever we think of Jonah we think of his being swallowed whole by a great fish (the Bible makes no mention of a whale). The story of how he was swallowed by a fish is a long one, but basically he was trying to escape from the mission God gave him to preach repentance to the Assyrians. You need to know that the Assyrians were an especially warlike, aggressive, merciless people who lived on the Tigris River, 250 miles north of Baghdad. The Assyrians had already destroyed most of Israel by the time Jonah was written, so you can imagine there was deep hatred on the part of the Jews for the Assyrians. Jonah was three days in the belly of the fish before he was spit out on the shore of Assyria. Having learned he couldn't run away from God, Jonah decided he had better do what God wanted. The story about Jonah that we hear in our first reading today is more amazing than the part of the story about the fish. Without miracles or spectacular signs, Jonah preached a one line, unenthusiastic warning to the people of Nineveh and in one day converted the entire city of Nineveh. To get an idea of how astonishing this would be, think of an unknown individual showing up in Baghdad today and in one day every person, including all the terrorists, repenting and converting to Christianity. Would that be something or what!!!

Today's reading shows God is not interested in punishing people but in giving all people, even the bad guys, a chance to reform. The passage sets the theme for the gospel when Jesus began his public ministry by preaching repentance. We know from real life experience and from the experience Jesus and the Apostles had, calling people to change their lives is not as easy as the story of Jonah makes it appear to be.

HOMILY – This week the mayor of New Orleans, acting like an Old Testament prophet, said (and I quote): "Surely God is mad at America. He sent us hurricane after hurricane after hurricane, and it's destroyed and put stress on this country." He added: "... surely he (God) is upset at black America also." Whenever something bad happens many people, like a knee jerk reaction, like to say "God must be punishing us." If the mayor of New Orleans had received a true anointing to be God's prophet, he would have warned people ahead of time and not just after the fact. The picture of God that the mayor of New Orleans paints, as an angry God punishing us because we've been bad, is not the picture of the God I know. Even God in the Old Testament often pictured as a God of wrath, is interested in saving people, not in destroying them; for example, in our first reading God sent Jonah to warn the cruel and warlike people of Nineveh so they would not be destroyed. Why are there hurricanes and natural disasters? I think it's just part of living on a planet that is constantly adjusting to natural forces. And maybe we are making things worse by the way we abuse our environment. However, there are times when bad things do happen because we do not do what God wants. We have a God who wants only good things for us and for that reason he tells us how we should live in order to guide us to what is best for us. And when we ignore him, we only cause problems for ourselves.

This is why God sent his Son to us, to teach us and guide us. "The time has come," he said as he began his public ministry. "The Kingdom of God is near. Turn away from your sins and believe in this good news." As we heard in today's gospel, Jesus needed help to announce this good news so he started choosing people who would help him.

Jesus said "I came that they may have life and may have it to the full." Jesus' teachings are good news. Sometimes, though, it doesn't feel that way. Forgiving people who have hurt us, loving our enemies, getting up on Sunday morning when we're tired, keeping the commandments, giving some of our hard earned money to others; sometimes it doesn't feel like good news. That's why he said, "believe in this good news," because we don't always feel it.

Turn away from sin is part of his message. "Turn away from sin" is the translation of a word from the Greek: which means a change of mind. Generally it is translated repentance or conversion. Jesus is telling us if we're going to start believing in what he tells us we have to change our mind, to stop thinking and believing and doing what we used to.

Of course the reason we are here is because we do believe in Christ. But unless there's a Mother Theresa among us, I suspect there is room for improvement in most of us. Jesus' call to conversion is sort of like New Year's resolutions. We make New Year's resolutions because we realize we can do better, we can be better, we have more potential than we are using.

Until we hopefully reach heaven where we will be perfect, there'll always be room for improvement, always be some areas of our lives where the gospel of Jesus has not yet penetrated. Would that conversion were as easy as the book of Jonah pictures it. If it were, we wouldn't have to be reminded of it so often. Amen.

4th Sunday in Ordinary Time
February 1, 2015

INTRODUCTION – (*Deuteronomy 18, 15-20; I Cor. 7, 32-35; Mark 1, 21-28*) Our second reading from Paul's letter to the Corinthians might be difficult to understand. So I would like to give a little background. The passage is from a section of Paul's letter where he is dealing with a question about **marriage and celibacy**. Paul began this topic by affirming the value of marriage and then he moves on, which is today's reading, to affirm the value of celibacy. His suggestion (not a rule), is directed to those who were not yet married or who were widowed and he points out the advantages of remaining unmarried. This suggestion is based on the expectation of the early Church that Jesus was going to return very soon and with his coming the world would come to an end. To quote what Paul said in last week's reading: "the time is running out" and "the world as we know it is passing away." If it seems as if Paul is overemphasizing the spiritual advantages of celibacy, consider how you might view things with regard to getting married and starting a family if you seriously thought that probably in a year or two the world would end and Jesus would return.

Some background about our first reading might also be helpful. It takes place on the East side of the Jordan River across from the Promised Land. After many years in the desert, God's people were ready to cross the Jordan and enter the land God promised to give them. Moses knew that very soon God would call him to leave this world and God's people would cross the Jordan and enter their new Land without him. Basically Moses is saying "goodbye." He assures them God would not leave them without direction or leadership. God would send them another prophet like himself who would speak God's word to them. We usually think of a prophet as a person who foretells the future, and sometimes the prophet did, but the best definition of a prophet is at the end of today's first reading: one who speaks God's word. Our first reading prepares us for the gospel where Jesus speaks God's word with power and authority.

HOMILY – From the very beginning of Mark's gospel, Mark wants us to know who Jesus is. He introduced his gospel with the words: "the beginning of the gospel of Jesus Christ, the Son of God." Eight verses later John the Baptist testifies that Jesus would baptize with the Holy Spirit. Three verses after that Jesus is baptized and God in Heaven speaks to Jesus: "You are my beloved Son. With you I am well pleased." If we read down a few more verses, to verse 24, Mark again tells us about Jesus. This information comes from a very unexpected source, the devil, who acknowledges Jesus as "the Holy One of God." The people in the synagogue are impressed with the power in Jesus' teaching and they consider him a prophet; but the evil spirit already knows who Jesus is. By the way, this is the first miracle mentioned by St. Mark. He not only wants us to know who Jesus is but he wants us to know Jesus was not afraid of the evil powers in this world and was willing to face them head on.

When we were in catechism class, we were taught that temptations come from the world, the flesh and the devil. We've all experienced how the world and the flesh can lead us astray, but many people think of the devil as a myth. In my 50 years as a priest, I am convinced through the daily news and through counseling I have done that devils are for real. Devils are smart enough **not** to make themselves obvious.

That way they can work more effectively because we are not aware that they are busy doing their thing. I believe that Jesus' experience with demons was also real. I would grant that years ago epilepsy or mental illness was considered to be caused by demons, but I believe in other cases, it was the real thing Jesus was fighting against. Exorcisms make up the largest single category of healings in the gospels of Matthew, Mark, and Luke. I have two last points.

1) Jesus is admired by many people today. He is considered a good person, a person who cared greatly about others and a great teacher. The Moslems even consider him a great prophet. But that's **all** he is in the minds of many people. We, as Christians, see him differently. He is not someone whom we can choose to follow or ignore depending on whether we agree with him or not. He is the Holy One of God; he is God's Son. When he speaks to us, we must listen to him. That's one of the reasons why we come to Mass on Sunday. The whole first part of the Mass focuses on hearing God's word and reflecting on it.

2) The devil: We don't hear much about the devil except in jokes. But the devil is not a joke. The Scriptures take him seriously. I have mentioned that in my experience as a priest and counselor, I definitely have come to believe there are evil powers at work in the world, which are called devils. I've never had any dramatic experiences like in today's gospel or like the movie *The Exorcist*, which, by the way was, in most respects, based on a true story. Here's why I think most of us are not aware of the devil's strategy, it's because the devil approaches us from where we are the weakest. The devil is very subtle. For example, if we're angry, the devil simply encourages us to keep feeling that way, and the devil may even suggest additional reasons why we

should be boiling with anger. The same goes with other weaknesses, such as hatred, envy, laziness, pride, lust, greed, gluttony, etc. There is one stronger than the devil who will help us if we ask. He is a prophet greater than Moses – he is the Holy One of God and is God's Son. Ask his help in time of temptation. Amen.

5th Sunday in Ordinary Time
February 8, 2015

INTRODUCTION – (*Job 7,1-4.6-7; 1 Corinthians 9,16-19.22-23; Mark 1,29-39*) We hear from Job in our first reading. He had been a prosperous and happy man. Then suddenly he lost everything; hostile tribes destroyed his cattle, his sheep, his camels and his workers. A violent wind collapsed the house where his children were gathered for a meal and it killed them all at once. Soon after, Job's health began to deteriorate and his skin was covered with sores. He laments: "I shall not see happiness again." Job, who was always faithful to God, complained God was being unfair to him. At the time this book was written, the pervading belief among the Jews was that if we are good, God will bless us, and if we're not good, all kinds of terrible things will happen to us. At the same time the Jews were beginning to discover that life doesn't always work that way. Like Job we still struggle to answer the question of why good people suffer? The gospel is in contrast with the pathetic story of Job where we see Jesus at work trying to lessen people's sufferings by his many exorcisms and healings.

Contrary to Job who is deeply depressed, St. Paul, in today's second reading, is full of enthusiasm with his ministry of preaching the gospel. He's not doing it because he wants to get rich (actually, for the most part he provided for his own needs, working as a tentmaker).

He is using himself as an example for the Corinthians to follow in teaching them to unselfishly serve God and lovingly serve one another.

HOMILY – Our readings today deal with one of the deepest mysteries of life, the problem of why good people suffer. It makes sense to most people that if someone is evil, and bad things happen to them, we say, well they deserved it. When someone doesn't seem to deserve it we ask "why?" Some people quietly judge "that person must have done something really bad to deserve what happened to them!" That's what Job's friends thought about Job. They told him "Job, you must have some hidden sin or you wouldn't be suffering like you are." Job protested that he didn't deserve what was happening to him. The book of Job goes on for 42 chapters trying to understand the problem of suffering. Was the Book of Job ever a true story? I believe it was and in a sense it is a true story of thousands of other people who lived or are living a life similar to Job's.

Our problem is that we believe in a God who can do anything and we believe in a God who is fair and just. We figure if God can do anything, why doesn't he help good people who are suffering? This is the mystery. In the Book of Job, the author, after struggling for 42 chapters to understand the problem of suffering, resolved it eventually by telling us that God heard Job's complaint and restored all of his property - giving him back twice the wealth he previously enjoyed. God gave Job three beautiful daughters who produced many grandchildren for him. Many readers of Job might say "that's great for Job, but I don't see something like that happening very often."

We see in the gospel Jesus' answer to suffering; he helped everyone who came to him for healing. Any town he visited would have loved to hold on to Jesus so he could keep everyone in town healthy. Jesus' agenda wasn't just to be a famous healer. He came to be our teacher; he came with a message intended for the whole world; he came to save us by giving his life for us. Jesus healed people wherever he was, and he sent his apostles out to heal as well. Jesus had to stay on the move so he could bring his message of forgiveness and love and salvation to as many people as possible.

When Jesus or his apostles did heal people, he showed us something about how God feels about suffering. God cares about us and he's with us in our suffering. He is not only with us, he even suffered for us. That care about those who suffer has continued on among Jesus' followers. Jesus' followers have always prayed for the sick and at times Jesus' healing power showed itself through those prayers. Wikipedia said "in-patient medical care, in the sense of what we today consider a hospital, was an innovation driven by Christian mercy." This innovation came about once Christians were allowed to practice their faith publicly under the Emperor Constantine.

The story of God caring about our suffering, Jesus' willingness to suffer for us, and the readiness of his followers to care for those who are suffering does not end here. God promised to put an end to suffering altogether for those who have chosen to believe in him and to follow him. As Isaiah says so beautifully: "then the eyes of the blind shall see, and the ears of the deaf be opened; then the lame shall leap like a stag, and the mute tongue sing for joy." (Is. 35, 5-6)

The resurrection of Jesus shows us what God has planned for those who love him. In the resurrection, Christ has triumphed over sin and death and he invites us to share in his victory. He only asks that we follow him and trust him. His resurrection, for those who believe, proves what St. Paul tells us, that "for those who love God, all things work out for the best." That's one of the verses from Paul that keeps me going. Amen.

6th Sunday in Ordinary Time
February 12, 2006

INTRODUCTION – (*Leviticus 13, 1-2. 44-46; 1 Corinthians 13, 31 – 11, 1; Mark 1, 40-45*) There are two chapters in the book of Leviticus on how to deal with leprosy. Many skin diseases in those days were lumped together under the diagnosis of leprosy. Quite possibly the person we hear about in today's gospel had ringworm, a type of a fungus. So many diseases of the skin were contagious that the person with such a disease had to be isolated from the community. It was not as humane as our isolation wards in the hospital. Actually they had to live outside the city and community, away from friends, family and their occupation. Usually they ended up living in caves or tombs. It was the priest's job to decide if a person was infected with this dreaded disease and if it seemed that a person's skin cleared up the priest had to pronounce that the person could re-enter society. Today in our first reading we hear a small section from the book of Leviticus that describes how to deal with a variety of skin diseases they referred to as leprosy. It prepares us for the gospel where Jesus was not afraid to touch a person infected with a skin disease, which would have made him unclean; but in touching the man he gave him back not only his health, but restored him to his home, his family and friends, his synagogue and his occupation.

HOMILY – I announced that today I would anoint the sick after Mass. I thought it was a good day to offer this sacrament because the gospel was about Jesus healing someone. However, in view of the weather, probably many of the people who would have come to be anointed decided to stay home. But there will be other opportunities after the weather turns a little warmer.

I administer the anointing of the sick to everyone I visit in the hospital or nursing home or to anyone I visit who is a shut-in. I make use of it frequently. I believe in the power of prayer and I believe in the power of this sacrament for the sick.

Recently I anointed a friend of mine who was going into the hospital. He was brought up in the old school when this sacrament was called Extreme Unction and he was a bit shocked when I suggested giving him the anointing. I don't think my explanation that this is a prayer and sacrament for the sick gave him much reassurance, because after I left him, he told his friends "I just received the last rites!" He might have thought he was a goner, but he wasn't. He's quite healthy today. It was the Second Vatican Council that restored this sacrament to its original purpose: a prayer and sacrament for healing. Healing was part of Jesus' mission and also that of the disciples. When Jesus sent his disciples to help him in his work, St. Mark tells us they preached that people should turn away from their sins, they cast out demons and anointed many with oil and healed them. Even when physical healing is not the outcome, there is always some unique blessing and grace that comes with the sacrament.

Science had been pretty skeptical about faith and prayer until recently. Prayer is one of the liveliest areas of research in the field of alternative medicine today. For the past 15 or 20 years, science has started looking upon prayer more positively. Ten years ago Dr. Larry Dossey, a surgeon from Texas who didn't believe much in prayer for healing, started reviewing all the research on it and he ended up writing the book Healing Words. He concluded that prayer should be included with the prescriptions doctors write. An example of a more recent study was reported in October last year in Prevention Magazine. Dr. Mitchel Krucoff, a cardiologist at Duke University did a study with 150 men with heart problems. He concluded that, compared with a control group, those who were prayed for had a 50% reduction in heartbeat abnormalities and a 100% reduction in clinical outcomes such as heart attacks and heart failure. And none of the patients, their families, or the doctors treating them knew who was in the group being prayed for. I could bore you with other studies, but these studies appeal to the scientific side of my personality, because although I have faith in the power of prayer, I also had a good background in the scientific method when I studied experimental psychology. So when I tell you prayer works, it's not just from what I believe, it's not just from what I have personally experienced (and I have had many personal experiences of the power of prayer), but I can support it from scientific research. It works. At the same time it is mysterious. We can't always control the outcome. And most of all, it doesn't happen as fast as we would like or as fast as it happens in the gospels. One thing Jesus kept telling us over and over is to keep praying, to keep knocking. I think when we give up too soon, it shows we don't have very much faith in what prayer has the power to do for us. And we have to remember, when we pray, we are not dealing with inert substances, like using antibiotics to cure a bacterial infection. When we pray we are talking to our God whose wisdom and love is infinitely beyond our own. "Sometimes, God's operating from a larger script than yours," Dr. Frederick Flach says. Prayers are answered in many ways. On some occasions God may use illness for a purpose we do not understand. On other occasions, God may intervene directly and on still other occasions God may work through others, especially health care professionals. Although I've seen prayer bring immediate results, more times than not, it works better when we don't give up praying but keep at it. Keep knocking with faith. "Lord, if you want to, you can cure me."

1st Sunday of Lent
February 22, 2015

INTRODUCTION – (*Genesis 9, 8-15; I Peter 3, 18-22; Mark 1, 12-15*) I want to call your attention to the word "covenant" in today's first reading. This important concept will dominate our first readings every week during Lent this year. Typically "covenants" were quite common centuries ago. They were somewhat similar to what we call a "contract" today. A "covenant" was a serious commitment or promise two parties (be they individuals or nations) made to each other. It defined the relationship and the expectations they had of one another. The word "covenant" is not in common use today except when people speak of the marriage covenant. (We also hear it at the consecration of the wine during Mass.) When God chose to enter into a relationship with his people, he made a covenant with them. He promised what he would do and told them what he expected of them. Today we hear about the covenant God made with Noah and with all of creation after the great flood. Notice this covenant is unusual in that God promises what he will do for his people while he asks nothing of his people in return. St. Peter, in the second reading, tells us the covenant God made with Noah and his family prefigured baptism which is God's pledge to us of salvation and eternal life.

HOMILY – In our relations with God, there are moments of joy, moments when we feel God's love and presence, and there are moments when we feel no comfort or consolation at all. I suspect Jesus went through such times too. In the section of the gospel, right before today's gospel, we are told that when Jesus was baptized, the Spirit came down upon him like a dove and God's voice spoke from heaven: "you are my beloved Son; with you I am well pleased." Wouldn't you assume that was a high moment for Jesus? Then the gospel tells us (which is today's passage) at once the Spirit drove him out into the wilderness where he would be for forty days fasting and praying. The excitement of the baptism was followed by, what I would suspect, was a long period of dryness. Most of us are familiar with the three temptations Matthew and Luke tell us about, but our gospel today is from Mark who says simply that he was tempted by Satan. The Greek word tempted can also mean he was tested by Satan - sort of a test of strength or endurance or fidelity and Jesus won the battle.

I think the test Jesus went through involved whether he would stay faithful to God's plan for him, a plan that would have very difficult times. Examples of some of the tests Jesus would have to go through could have been something like this: He could have chosen to use his special powers to his own advantage, like turning stones into bread when he was hungry, or for that matter, turning stones into gold when the apostles were out of money - but he didn't. He could have used his special powers to gain influence and popularity and prestige; some of the people who knew him wanted to make him their king, but he didn't agree. He could have walked away from those who came to arrest him in the Garden of Gethsemane, but he didn't. We can only speculate what Jesus experienced or thought about during those 40 days. We can assume that the presence of Satan, the forty days of fasting, and the arrest of John the Baptist foreshadowed, from the start, Jesus' proclamation of the kingdom would encounter major obstacles.

The example of Jesus is presented to us today to encourage us to always remain faithful to God especially during difficult times and to make the next 40 days a special time for ourselves to turn more to God. Getting to Church this past Wednesday to get ashes and to begin this Lenten season was difficult because of the weather. But if you missed Mass Wednesday, there is nothing stopping you from making the next 40 days a holy time, a time to pray a little more, a time to think more about God's goodness and love and about loving him more and loving each other more genuinely.

2nd Sunday of Lent
March 1, 2015

INTRODUCTION – (*Genesis 22:1-2,9,10-13,15-18; Romans 8:31-34; Mark 9:2-10*) Last week we heard about God's covenant with Noah; God promised he would never again cause a flood that would destroy all life on earth. The sign of that covenant is the rainbow. Sometime roughly 1750 years before Christ, God entered into another important covenant with a person named Abram. God promised Abram numerous blessings and many descendants. In return, God asked Abram simply to trust him. Today we hear how Abram (whose name has by now been changed to Abraham) remained trusting in a most difficult situation. By the way, Mt. Moriah is right in the center of Jerusalem where the Dome of the Rock now stands. That's the same place where Solomon built the Temple.

HOMILY – Roughly the first half of St. Mark's gospel tells us of Jesus' ministry of teaching and healing in Galilee. Before Jesus began his ministry, however, he was baptized by John the Baptist. At Jesus' baptism the Spirit came down upon him like a dove and a voice came from the heavens which said: "you are my beloved Son, with you I am well pleased." As we heard in last Sunday's gospel, immediately the Spirit drove Jesus into the wilderness where he fasted and prayed for 40 days.

Today's gospel is from chapter nine in St. Mark and we are just a little past the half way point in Mark. Mark is preparing to tell us about Jesus' final days and his suffering and death. At the beginning of his gospel, we hear God the Father speak out about his beloved Son. On this occasion Jesus took his three closest apostles up to the top of Mt. Tabor, a mountain about 2000 feet high, and while there, Jesus' appearance began to change. The apostles saw Jesus' true identity and the glory that was always hidden by his human flesh. As before, the voice of the heavenly Father speaks: "This is my beloved Son. Listen to him." The three apostles were terrified and yet this ecstatic moment prompted them to want to pitch tents so they could remain there for a while - if not permanently.

It was not to be. Jesus' ministry was not finished, and it would not be finished until after his death and resurrection. Jesus told them not to tell anyone about this vision until after he had risen from the dead.

Like the apostles, we prefer to picture Jesus in glory, but we can't forget Jesus is still our God even as he was hanging on the cross in extreme agony. Our God could not suffer in his divinity, so he took on our human nature to share our suffering and so he could give his life for us. We must meet our God under both aspects - as our suffering Lord and as our glorified Lord. It is in meeting him under both aspects that we are more able to deal with the suffering that comes our way in our journey through life. Coming to Mass each week keeps us in touch with Jesus' sacrifice of his body and blood and it gives us the promise of future glory. Lent too can help us continue to be aware of what Jesus did for us. Amen.

3rd Sunday of Lent
March 8, 2015

INTRODUCTION – (*Exodus 20, 1-17; I Corinthians 1, 22-25; John 2, 13-25*) Covenant is a theme that keeps recurring in our first reading these Sundays of Lent. The first Sunday of Lent, we hear about God's covenant with Noah. Last Sunday we heard about God's covenant with Abraham and how Abraham's trust in God was tested when he heard God tell him to sacrifice his son. Today, the third Sunday of Lent, we hear about God's covenant with his people as they traveled under the leadership of Moses from slavery in Egypt to the Promised Land. Typically a covenant had two parts, what each party to the covenant promised they would do for one another. God, for his part of the covenant, had promised his people liberty, land, prosperity and his special care and love. Today's first reading tells us what God expected of his people in return.

HOMILY – Fortunately, I do not have to talk about money very often. Typically, once a year I inform the parish how we are doing financially: whether we are doing well or falling short. Today is entirely different. I'm not going to talk about how we as a parish are doing, but how we as an Archdiocese are doing. It is not just how we have done the past year, but how we hope to be doing years from now. I could call my topic an investment in the future: will Catholic schools still be around, will we have enough money to support our many retired priests, will we be able to keep the seminary going and will we be able to really reach out to the poor and help them to have enough to eat and provide programs for them to improve their lives. Add all this up, and this is a big endeavor. Our Archbishop is taking his responsibilities seriously and is responding to some of the needs we have as an archdiocese. We do have to realize that the Church is not just St. Boniface in Northside, but it is world-wide. Sometimes we take up collections for foreign missions, for retired religious, for the Holy Land, for the charitable work of the Holy Father, for respect of life, etc. These special collections remind us of the universality of the Church. Our focus today though is on the southwest corner of Ohio where there are almost a half million Catholics living in cities like Piqua, Sidney, Troy, Minster, Springfield, Dayton, Hamilton, Hillsboro, Lebanon, and especially Cincinnati. The Archbishop is responsible for all of this and is asking for our help. He is very shrewd financially and I trust his judgment 100%.

The last time we had a big, archdiocesan drive like this one was when I graduated from high school – back in 1955, about 60 years ago. At that time Archbishop Alter was the Archbishop and he was interested mainly in building a few high schools. It was an investment that is still paying dividends. So we are talking about serious money today.

It hasn't escaped me that there is something ironic about reading the gospel about Jesus cleansing the Temple and my asking for a significant donation from each of our parishioners. I might comment that there were many abuses at the time of Jesus regarding Temple worship. We read that Jesus drove noisy and messy large animals out of the Temple like sheep and oxen. Matthew tells us the Temple had been turned into a den of thieves. The Jewish historian Josephus informs us that the High Priest, who no doubt benefitted from all these dealings, was "the great procurer of money." It is possible too that Jesus' action indicated that the time had come for the Jews to no longer sacrifice animals for Jesus was about the offer the perfect sacrifice. There was also the belief that the Messiah would build a new Temple and this could have been the meaning of this prophetic act of Jesus. At any event, until Jesus teaches us how to multiply loaves and fishes and how to change water into wine, we're going to need money or its equivalent in order to do the Lord's work and to survive.

So I wish to talk for a few minutes about the One Faith, One Hope, One Love capital campaign. Every church in the Archdiocese is participating, and every church will attempt to invite each of its parishioners to participate. The overall goal for the whole Archdiocese is $130 million. Our goal at St. Boniface is $570 thousand. This figure is computed from what people give in the collection on Sundays. I told a friend that's how it was figured and he responded, "I'm glad I didn't give very much in the collection." I'm not recommending that attitude to anyone. Two months ago when I was getting started organizing this campaign, $570 thousand seemed impossible, but since then, after contacting a couple of dozen people, we already have pledges totaling about $266 thousand. We're already almost half way there. I think our goal is doable and it is very heartening to me that our people have started off being so supportive.

I briefly touched on the purposes of the campaign earlier. I want to expand on that a little more. A couple of weeks ago, you received in the bulletin a pie chart like this. You were probably wondering what it was. Well, now you know. It indicates that half of the campaign money will go toward Catholic schools. One of the most important jobs of the Church is to teach and Catholic schools have been an effective way to do that. A percent of the campaign will go toward the seminary and toward recruiting vocations. Another percent will help provide funds for our retired diocesan priests, while another percent goes for helping the poor through Catholic charities and social services. Lastly, 20% of the funds will be returned to our parish, which the Parish Council thought could best be spent to enlarge our lower parking lot. That means if we meet our goal of $570 thousand, over $100 thousand will come back to St. Boniface. I think it's obvious that any Church without adequate parking is bound to lose parishioners.

This Thursday, if we don't have snow, we will have a meeting that will expand a lot more on each of these items. The meeting will be for those who might be able to help us contact other parishioners, but if you come to the meeting you will save yourself having to be called on personally, to have someone explain the program to you. If you go to the meeting and you are contacted you can say I went to the meeting and $XXX is what I pledge and fill out a pledge card.

I think this is enough said for now. I hope everyone will join me in supporting this very important program for the good of the Archdiocese and for the good of our Church. Thank you for your patient listening.

4th Sunday of Lent
March 15, 2015

INTRODUCTION – (*2 Chronicles 36, 14-16.19-23; Ephesians 2, 4-10; John 3, 14-21*) Last Sunday we heard about God's covenant with his people as they traveled with Moses from slavery in Egypt to freedom in the Promised Land. God promised his people many blessings and his special love and in return they were to keep his

Law, especially the part of the Law we call "The Ten Commandments." The Jewish historian who wrote the book of Chronicles gives us a summary of over seven centuries of infidelities on the part of God's people to their covenant. The consequences of their infidelity led to untold disaster for the nation, but God would not let them be totally destroyed. Just to help you visualize this better, the Babylonians who practically destroyed them came out of modern day Iraq. The Persians who restored them to their land came out of Iran. Our psalm refrain is the lament of God's people as they suffered captivity in Babylon. Next week we will hear Jeremiah promise that God would make a new covenant with his people since the people observed the old one so poorly. We celebrate and renew God's new covenant as always as we celebrate the Eucharist today.

HOMILY – St. John's gospel is the only gospel that mentions Nicodemus. We just heard about him today at the beginning of John's gospel. He was a Pharisee and a Jewish religious leader, which implies he was one of the 71 members of the Sanhedrin, the supreme ruling council of the Jews.

In the room off the vestibule in the back of church, we have a stained glass window picturing Nicodemus talking with Jesus. That room is usually referred to as the brides' room, but originally it was the baptistery. It is fitting that the stained glass window in the baptistery should picture Nicodemus because at their first meeting, Jesus told Nicodemus a person cannot enter God's kingdom unless they are born again of water and the Spirit, which is a reference to baptism.

Nicodemus came to Jesus at night. Nicodemus was being practical, of course, for the supreme ruling council of the Jews had only hatred for Jesus. Nicodemus may have feared he would lose many of his good friends if he were caught having a normal conversation with Jesus. John's gospel is also speaking on a symbolic level. In telling us Nicodemus came to Jesus at night, John is telling us Nicodemus was far from having complete faith in Jesus. Since Jesus is the true light who gives light to all people, as John told us earlier in his gospel, Nicodemus hasn't found that light yet. He's still in the dark - only searching for the light.

Today's gospel is one of the most popular and beloved passages in the entire Bible: "God so loved the world that he gave his only Son, so that everyone who believes in him may not perish but may have eternal life." (John 3,16)

Too many people think that to believe in Jesus, all we have to do is say the words: "I believe in Jesus, or I believe he is the Son of God." Believing in Jesus is much more than that. To believe in Jesus is to live the way he taught us; i.e., to live in his light. Any other way of living is to live in darkness. To believe in Jesus is to believe he has come down from heaven (Jn. 3,13) so he could teach us about heavenly things. To believe in Jesus is to believe he is our spiritual nourishment. He told us: "I am the living bread that came down from heaven" (Jn. 6, 35. 51); it is to believe that he is the "good shepherd" (Jn 10,11.14); that he is "the resurrection and the life" (Jn. 11,25); that he is the "real vine" and we are branches who draw our life from him (Jn 15,1.5) and that he is "the way, the truth, and the life." (Jn 14,6) To say I believe in Jesus is basically to turn our life over to God.

At this point in the gospel Nicodemus is still in the dark unable to grasp the spiritual lessons Jesus is trying to teach him. Nicodemus had a mind and heart that was seeking to know the truth and coming to Jesus was the best place to begin. Later in the gospel of John we hear about Nicodemus again. The supreme council of the Jews is discussing Jesus and Nicodemus argues that Jesus deserves a fair trial before he is condemned. Nicodemus was rebuffed for his remarks. The third time Nicodemus shows up is at Jesus' burial. He came with 75 or 100 pounds of spices with which Jesus would be embalmed. At this point we see Nicodemus had moved beyond his fear and made a 100% commitment to Jesus, Even though he had watched Jesus die as a condemned criminal, he made this commitment without wavering. That took real faith. He could see in his heart that when Jesus was lifted up on the cross it was really Jesus being lifted up into glory. May our Lenten practices help us to grow in our faith and in our total commitment to Jesus. Amen.

5th Sunday of Lent
March 22, 2015

INTRODUCTION – (*Jeremiah 31,31-35; Hebrews 5,7-9; John 12,20-33*) The prophet Jeremiah lived 600 years before Christ. He was sent by God on a mission of mercy to warn God's people that they were living on the edge of a catastrophe. If they didn't start following God's ways, the Babylonians would invade their land and destroy them. Centuries of wanton idolatry, social injustice and even human sacrifice had seriously weakened the moral fiber of God's people. God was telling them through the prophet Jeremiah how they could avoid disaster. Of course, they ignored Jeremiah and persecuted him for his message. Today's first reading comes shortly before the Babylonian invasion. Centuries earlier, God had made a covenant with his people through Moses and the people continually violated it. In spite of their unfaithfulness, God still loved his people and he promised he would make a new covenant with them as the former one did not work out so well. Six hundred years later, Jesus used these words, "new covenant" when he gave the cup of his blood to his disciples at the Last Supper. We renew that covenant with him each time we come to Mass.

HOMILY – The setting for today's gospel is that Jesus is in Jerusalem. It is springtime, just a few days before the Jewish Passover. In just a few days, Judas will betray Jesus and Jesus will be arrested, condemned and put to death. When some Greeks showed up asking to "see" Jesus (another way of saying they wanted some time with him), Jesus knew that his ministry exclusively among the Jewish people had come to an end, that his death was imminent and it was time for the Apostles to go outside the Jewish world and to preach the gospel of God's love to everyone. Jesus uses the word "hour" quite often in John's gospel. His "hour" always referred to his death, resurrection and his return to the Father. Jesus says, the "hour has come for the Son of Man to be glorified." (Jn. 12, 23)

Always at this time of year, there is someone who asks "Why did Jesus have to die?" Philosophers, theologians and saints have puzzled over the answer to these questions. Of course, I have always wondered why it had to happen. I'll tell you how I answered it to my own satisfaction, but I'm sure there is much more to it than what I could figure out. I believe that Jesus' death was the consequence of his ministry of fighting against evil wherever or whenever he saw it. In his fight against evil, he had to buck up against the powerful Jewish leaders, he had to teach people to forgive, to love, to help the poor, to be pure, not to be prejudiced - in brief, to put God's will above their own wants and desires. If Jesus tried to save his life and run away and hide, his whole ministry would die, his apostles would go back to fishing or whatever they were occupied with before he called them. All the work he did, all his teaching would be forgotten. Maybe if he taught and preached for 45 years like the Buddha, or 40 years like Moses, or 22 years like Mohammed, some people would have remembered some of what he said or did, but Jesus' public ministry was for only three years. So he knew that in preaching the message of God's love that the Father had sent him to preach, he had to remain faithful to his work until the end. Seeing it that way helps me see why Jesus had to die. Jesus knew, moreover, that his work would not end with his death. Did he not say, "destroy this temple (meaning his body) and in three days I will raise it up"? He uses two images in today's gospel to tell us his death would bear much fruit and it would save all who would believe in him.

Jesus said his death would be like a seed that is planted. Think what happens when a seed is planted. It springs to life and produces many more seeds like itself. Jesus' death and resurrection would form the beginning of the Christian community. Many more people would be filled with his spirit, his attitude of love and obedience for God the Father, and his love for others.

There is another image Jesus uses in today's gospel to explain his death. It is an image borrowed from the Old Testament. I would like to spend a moment explaining it because I think most people are unfamiliar with it. While the Jews were traveling with Moses after leaving Egypt, they came across an area infested with seraph serpents. Seraph means fiery, which implies that their bite must have been very painful. Many Jews died from the serpents' poisonous bite. The people saw this as punishment from God for their constant complaining, and they came to Moses and asked him to pray for their forgiveness. Moses did and God told him to fabricate a bronze serpent and put it up on a staff. If anyone was bitten by a serpent all they had to do was to look at the bronze serpent and they would be healed. (*Numbers 21, 6-9*) Jesus' death, resurrection and return to the Father would be a lifting up, meaning both his physical lifting up on the cross and his glorification at the right hand of the Father. This lifting up in death and glory would draw all people to him - at least all people who turn to him in faith, and they will be saved. This is the third time Jesus uses this image in John's gospel.

Those who see death as the end of everything are missing a very important teaching as we hear Jesus talk about his own death which is a source of life and salvation for those who believe in him. All this ties in with our first reading about a new covenant, for it is in his blood that Jesus makes a covenant with us, calling us to be faithful to him as he promises eternal life and salvation. Amen.

Palm Sunday of the Passion of the Lord
March 29, 2015

INTRODUCTION – (*Isaiah 50: 4-7; Psalm 22; Philippians 2: 6-11; Mark 14: 1-15:47*) Five hundred years before Christ, the prophet Isaiah tells us about a person who is called God's Servant. We do not have the name of this Servant, but from four passages, from brief to very lengthy, we have been given much information **about** the Servant. To quickly summarize what we are told, the Servant faithfully followed God's call to bring justice to the earth and light to the nations. It was a call that would bring great suffering to the Servant - inflicted upon him by the people he came to help. These Servant passages marvelously describe Jesus which makes it especially amazing that they were composed so many years before Jesus was born. Today's first reading is the first part of the third Servant Song. The first reading is followed by Psalm 22, a meditation on the sufferings of a just person. In this Psalm Jesus prayed as he hung on the cross: "My God, my God, why have you abandoned me."

HOMILY – I'm sure all of us were horrified by the crash of the Germanwings aircraft this week. The latest explanation is that it was a deliberate crash by the co-pilot, committing suicide and taking 150 others with him. If that is true, this is more than suicide, which in itself is not right. What the Germanwings' crash demonstrates was pure evil.

It demonstrates that there are those who come into this world who bring great pain and suffering to others. Then there are those who are just the opposite. They are a source of favors and blessings to those they associate with, even sometimes to the point of sacrificing their own desires and comfort for the good of another. Parents know what I'm talking about. Good parents do it all the time.

In our first reading today, we hear about God's Servant who sacrificed and who was even persecuted because he or she dedicated their life to serving others. Then there was Jesus. He is the ultimate example of what it means to love others. He could heal the sick, raise the dead, miraculously feed a huge crowd with one little boy's lunch. He would teach people the way of God, and he was persecuted for it – even to death.

This week is Holy Week. One of our teachers in school asked me what did Jesus do between Palm Sunday and Holy Thursday. My answer was that each day he came to the Temple and **taught**. At night he stayed roughly a mile away from Jerusalem in Bethany, across the Kidron Valley. I encourage you to come to our Holy Week services. If you cannot, perhaps you can spend some time reading the gospels. Read about the Last Supper and the crucifixion of Jesus. Or read about Jesus' teachings and let Jesus teach you. I might even humbly suggest reading my homily book where I have other homilies about Holy Week. They are sitting on the radiators – and they are free. Any of this reading will connect you more with the spirit of this week. Amen.

Holy Thursday
April 2, 2015

HOMILY – (*Exodus 12: 1-8,11-14; 1 Corinthians 11:23-26; John 13:1-15*) St. John tells us of Jesus' love for his own. Jesus loved them to the end. John likes to use words that have a double meaning. Here, in the Greek, loving them to the end means loving them to the fullest extent of his divine love and it also means loving them to the end of his life. John then contrasts Jesus' love with Judas who planned to betray Jesus. Judas has no love in his heart for he had chosen to follow the inspiration of Satan. Jesus doesn't reveal Judas' plans to the others at this moment, but he gives his disciples a demonstration of humble service and love by going to each one to wash their feet. I wonder whether Jesus thought his demonstration of love and service would help Judas to change his mind. It is a demonstration we all must learn from and remember. Every year on Holy Thursday we reenact the foot washing. After he was finished, Jesus said: "if I, the master and teacher, have washed your feet, you ought to wash one another's feet." We should serve one another humbly and lovingly. The message here seems to be quite clear. There's a great deal more in the foot washing that I want us to reflect on. This deeper meaning comes out in Peter's objection to Jesus washing his feet. Peter didn't understand why Jesus should wash his feet. Jesus said, "what I am doing, you do not understand now, but you will understand later." From the gospels we know that Peter was sometimes pretty dense in understanding what Jesus was saying or doing, but this act of humble service should have been obvious to anyone, even Peter. However, Jesus is saying there's more to it than you know right now. As a matter of fact, the foot washing is so important that without it a disciple loses his heritage with Jesus. The word "heritage" is translated as "inheritance" in the gospel we just heard. Jesus said Peter would lose his inheritance "**with me**." This is a definite clue that Jesus was talking about eternal life in the kingdom of heaven. And Peter would lose that if Jesus did not wash him. Notice Jesus does not say, "if you are not washed," but he said: "if **I** do not wash you." The foot washing is more than just an example to be imitated; it is a saving action of Jesus, an action of Jesus that makes it possible for the disciples to have eternal life with Jesus. Understanding this much, Peter now goes to the opposite extreme. He declares, "don't just wash my feet, but my head and my hands as well." Jesus said ,"no, Peter, you misunderstand. It's not the number of washings that are important, but it is what the foot washing symbolizes." This is the main point. What does it symbolize? It symbolizes Jesus' humbling himself to death on the cross, something Peter would not understand it until later after the resurrection.

Jesus performed this servile task to prophesy symbolically that he was about to be humiliated in death. Peter's objection, provoked by the foot washing, enabled Jesus to explain the saving necessity of this death; it would establish a person's heritage **with him** and it would cleanse them of sin. "Unless **I** wash you, you will not have inheritance with me." Jesus is telling us we need to participate in the saving power of his death for us if we hope to share in his eternal life. Unfortunately, not everyone chooses to participate in this saving power. Judas was not changed by the foot washing because Judas' heart was filled with the evil he was intending; he was not moved by the love Jesus extended toward him.

We participate in his saving death and resurrection through our humble service of one another, through faith and the Scriptures, through the sacraments, especially through the Eucharist, the sacrament which he gave us on the night before he died. We continue on as Jesus told us at the end of tonight's gospel: "As I have done for you, you should also do." Amen.

(*Thoughts from The Anchor Bible, the Gospel According to John XIII – XXI, by Ray Brown, pg 564 – 569*)

Good Friday
April 6, 2012

HOMILY – (*Isaiah 52:13–53:12, Hebrews 4:14-16; 5:7-9, John 18:1–19:42*) "We thought of him as stricken, as one smitten by God and afflicted. But he was pierced for our offenses, crushed for our sins; upon him was the chastisement that makes us whole, by his stripes we were healed."

These words of the prophet were written 500 years before Christ. They describe God's Servant who suffered, not for his own sins, but for those of others. This was a difficult concept for God's people to grasp back at that time. According to their theology, if a person was a good person, God rewarded them and if a person was a bad person, God punished them. Since they had no real understanding of heaven and hell at that time in history, they had to conclude that reward and punishment would come about in this life. Thus, the Servant we heard about in today's first reading, who was stricken and afflicted, was thought of as suffering for something evil he, the Servant (whoever it was) must have done. Thus the verse I quoted said: "We thought of him as stricken, as one smitten by God and afflicted" (as though he had been evil).

Another facet of their theology and a major part of their religious practice was offering sacrifices to God. Their sacrifice would be a lamb or an ox or usually another kind of food. The sacrifice they offered was meant to symbolize the gift of themselves to God – a gift they offered to give worship to God, or to ask for a special favor or to seek God's forgiveness for their sins. This made sense to them, that they could offer a sacrifice for something bad they had done hoping God would forgive them. The passage about the Servant introduces a new idea, the idea that someone could offer a sacrifice for the sins of another and make reparation for the evil someone else had done. This was hard for them to understand (hard for us to understand) that the Servant "was pierced for our offenses, crushed for our sins." The Servant's suffering was really serving as a sacrifice before God, and it would bring down God's blessings on his people.

This is a conclusion St. Paul came to about Jesus. Paul was initially a persecutor of those who accepted Jesus as their Savior and Messiah. He was involved in the killing of Stephan the first martyr. He persecuted the Church of God beyond measure and tried to destroy it. (*Gal. 1:13*) It was considered blasphemy that proclaimed faith in Jesus as Savior and Messiah. Jesus was, after all, a condemned criminal. The Book of Deuteronomy says, "God's curse rests on him who hangs upon a tree." (*Deut 21:23*) Thus the Jews believed that if God's curse was on

Jesus, how could he be considered their Savior and Messiah. But Paul discovered that Jesus became a "curse for us," (*Gal. 3:13*) and this is how he made that discovery. The risen Jesus appeared to him. It became obvious to Paul that Jesus was not a dead criminal but one uniquely blessed by God. If God had showed him such a unique favor, Jesus must have pleased God in a most unique way. God is not in the habit of bringing people back to life. Jesus did bring a few people back to life, but it was back to the life they had had before. But the risen Jesus enjoyed a life of glory. The Acts of the Apostles describe a Jesus who appeared to Paul in a brilliant light, brighter than the sun in midday. (*Acts 26:13*) Paul seems to have recognized that Jesus' death could not have been God's curse upon Jesus; it could not have been an accident; it could not have been a punishment for something evil; it had to have been a special blessing from God. It could only have resulted from Jesus' special obedience and love for God. Since, in the Jewish mind death came as the result of sin, Jesus must have borne the curse of death not for anything he had done, but for others. In other words, Jesus' death was a sacrifice for the sins of others. We are freed from our sins if we accept his sacrifice by faith and trust in Christ's death for our salvation. Jesus gave us sacraments, especially Baptism and the Eucharist, to enable us to participate in his saving death. So Paul, the zealous persecutor of the Church, became the zealous defender of the Church and the zealous Apostle and preacher of Jesus as Savior and Messiah. Central to his preaching was the death and resurrection of Jesus. He writes to the Corinthians: "When I came to you proclaiming the mystery of God, I did not come with lofty words or wisdom. For I resolved to know nothing while I was with you except Jesus Christ, and him crucified." (*1 Cor. 2:1-*

2)

This process of viewing Paul's thinking about Jesus' death and resurrection makes sense to me; it has helped me to understand Jesus' death a little better and, hopefully, it will help you too.

Let me end by quoting Isaiah once more: "We thought of him as stricken, as one smitten by God and afflicted. But he was pierced for our offenses, crushed for our sins; upon him was the chastisement that makes us whole, by his stripes we were healed."

(borrowed much from Professor Bart Ehrman in his series of lectures on *The New Testament*, produced by The Teaching Company, Lecture 14)

Easter Vigil & Easter
April 4/5, 2015

HOMILY – *(Acts 10:34, 37-43; Colossians 3: 1-4; John 20:1-9)* We just heard the conclusion to the gospel of St. Mark. There is one last verse that was not read which I wish to reflect on. After the angel told the women to tell Jesus' disciples and Peter: Jesus "is going before you to Galilee; there you will see him, as he told you," Mark concludes with this surprising statement: "Then they (the women) went out and fled from the tomb, seized with trembling and bewilderment. They said nothing to anyone, for they were afraid." (*Mk. 16,8*) Today we are celebrating the day that was and ever will be the most significant day in the history of our world. And that is to say a lot. Our world has seen a lot of changes, some wonderful, such as inventions that changed our ways of doing things and our ways of living; some not so wonderful, such as inventions that could wipe out an entire nation in a few seconds.

Some people might argue that Christmas is the most important day in history, when God's Son came into this world, but God's Son and all he did and taught would have been quickly forgotten without the resurrection. His disciples (who had the responsibility of proclaiming his name and his teachings) were afraid to say they had ever heard of Jesus after he was arrested. The women who followed him even to Calvary were sure his ministry was at an end when they came to put the finishing touches on his burial. The empty tomb and the angel that proclaimed, "he is not here. He has been raised," left them running from the tomb, trembling and bewildered. Mark leaves us bewildered when he ends his gospel by telling us "they said nothing to anyone, for they were afraid." A later editor or scribe added a few appearances of the risen Lord (borrowed from Luke and John) to the end of Mark's gospel in order for it not to end so abruptly. It was strange the way Mark ended his gospel without telling us about any of the appearances of Jesus as the other three gospels did. Surely Mark knew about the appearance of the risen Lord to his disciples for Mark was writing 30 to 40 years after Jesus died and rose. As soon as the Holy Spirit came upon the disciples 50 days after Easter, the apostles started preaching openly about Jesus' resurrection. And the earliest actual document we have about the resurrection and Jesus appearing to his followers was written by Paul to the Corinthians about 15 years before Mark was written.

Surely Mark has a purpose in ending his gospel so abruptly. He is telling us it's up to us to spread the good news about Jesus' resurrection.

Indeed the resurrection of Jesus was significant for Jesus and his followers 2000 years ago, but it is also significant for each one of us. Not only did Jesus rise and show us death did not have the last word in his short life, but the resurrection tells us death does not have the last word in any of our lives. God wants us to share in Jesus' resurrection and new life and to be with him forever. God has better plans for us than for us to live out our lives here in this world and then for it all to be ended. Jesus tells us in John 10,10: "I came so that they might have life and have it more abundantly." These words keep me going; they keep me full of hope; they keep me full of expectation even when very good friends pass away – and I am experiencing that more and more as I get older. Paul says clearly: "if we have died with Christ, we believe that we shall also live with him." The last words from the angel in today's gospel also say it clearly, "he goes before you."

Is today significant? It is central for everything we do. It is the basis for our hope for heaven; it is the reason I know Christ is in the Eucharist; it is the reason we attend Mass on Sunday; it is the reason why we try to live good lives. Thank you for coming today; thank you for your faith. My prayer is that we always live our lives with resurrection faith. Amen.

Second Sunday of Easter
April 12, 2015

INTRODUCTION – *(Acts 4: 32-35; 1 John 5:1-6; John 20:19-31)* As most of you know, the Acts of the Apostles was written by Luke, the same Luke that wrote the third gospel. Our first reading every Sunday, from now until the end of May, will be from the Acts. Luke tells us today about the early Christian community. It must have been very early in the life of the Church because everyone got along so harmoniously. Later on in the Acts, we find out that it wasn't long until their system of sharing all things in common began to fall apart. Paul's letters tell us about many problems Paul had in dealing with the Churches he founded that caused him great anxiety. But for a short time in the beginning, the early Church was of one mind and one heart.

HOMILY – Our gospel begins on Easter Sunday night. The disciples had learned in early morning that Jesus' body was gone and that he had already appeared to several people. Suddenly Jesus appeared to them. He showed them his wounds so they would know it was really he. So much could be said about this appearance and the second appearance a week later, but what I want to focus on today is that Jesus gave the disciples the power to forgive sins.

This is surely the reason why this Sunday is designated Divine Mercy Sunday. Jesus forgave sins and now his Apostles could do it by his power and in his name. This is exactly what "mercy" means. It means God is reaching out to save us, to lead us by his grace to the kingdom of heaven. I think the notion of mercy is misunderstood by many people today. They think it means God is going to bring everyone into heaven no matter how they lived their life here on earth. Jesus is very clear that there are those who choose not to receive God's mercy and forgiveness. All we have to do is look at some of Jesus' parables in Matthew, such as the unforgiving servant, the workers in the vineyard, the parable of the wedding feast, the ten virgins, the parable of the talents, the last judgment.

It's easy to understand what Jesus meant when he said: "whose sins you forgive are forgiven." It's more difficult to understand what he meant by "whose sins you retain are retained." From what I've read, the retaining of sins would refer to the teaching ministry of the Apostles, identifying what is or is not evil, and what will keep a person in spiritual darkness rather than leading them into Christ's light. So intent is Jesus on saving all people that he has given to mere human beings a power that belongs only to God. This is mercy in that God wants to share his love with us, but we must accept it. Our relationship with God cannot be one-sided. God has reached out to us in love and we must respond in love. If we choose not to respond, God's mercy cannot save us for it cannot change us. We thus condemn ourselves. As Jesus said: "God did not send his Son into the world to condemn the world, but that the world might be saved through him. Whoever believes in him will not be condemned, but whoever does not believe has already been condemned because he has not believed in the name of the only Son of God." (Jn. 3, 17-18) A lot of other Christian denominations do not accept the sacrament of reconciliation (aka confession). I think it makes complete sense in that it gives us extra assurance of God's mercy and forgiveness and, psychologically, it has the positive effect of helping us be relieved of our guilt when we have done wrong. One thing I sometimes run into is that people do not always experience the peace that reconciliation can bring us. They do not feel that peace, not because God hasn't forgiven them, but because they haven't forgiven themselves. We all make mistakes, we're all sinners, that's what comes with being human. When God forgives us, we have to forgive ourselves and stop beating ourselves up. When we keep beating ourselves up, that's an unhealthy form of pride at work - telling us we shouldn't have done the things we did. Humility is to accept ourselves as we are and trying to do better.

There's one last thing about mercy. St. Teresa of Avila mentions it. When we have experienced God's mercy and forgiveness, we need to be merciful and forgiving toward someone who has hurt us. Now I'm not talking about being in an abusive relationship which we should get away from if possible; I'm talking about the thoughtless, uncaring, catty comments that may come our way in the course of interacting with one another.

After all, we do pray forgive us our trespasses as we forgive those who trespass against us.

Well, I guess I've said enough about mercy – so I will practice what I preach and have mercy on you and say Amen.

Third Sunday of Easter
April 22, 2012

INTRODUCTION – (*Acts 3:13-15, 17-19; 1 John 2:1-5a; Luke 24:35-48*) In our first reading, there is no mention of a crippled man being healed by Peter and John, but this is the context of Peter's speech that we are about to hear from the Acts of the Apostles. A man, lame from birth, was brought to the Temple every day so he could beg for alms. Remember, in the Jewish mentality of the time, this man was not only physically impaired, but everyone would have looked upon him as a very sin-full person. The Jews would have thought that God was punishing him for something he or his parents must have done. A short time after the coming of the Spirit on Pentecost, Peter and John went to the Temple for afternoon prayer. The lame man saw them and asked for a little money. Peter said, "I don't have any money, but I will give you what I have. In the name of Jesus Christ of Nazareth, get up and walk." Then Peter helped him to his feet and he was healed. He was so excited, he jumped and danced and praised God. Of course, this created quite a commotion and everyone wondered what had happed. It was a perfect opportunity for Peter to explain the healing power of the risen Jesus. Notice Peter is very outspoken in accusing all of his Jewish listeners, not just their leaders, of rejecting Jesus and calling for his death. Peter said God can excuse them because they acted out of ignorance, but from now on they have no excuse, and they must repent and be converted for they had just seen the risen Jesus at work in the healing of the lame man. It is not the entire speech of Peter, but it is the most important part of it.

HOMILY – I came across an interesting parable the other day about an old pine tree. It was tall, 70 feet above the forest. Younger trees were also tall but none of them had a top as filled with foliage as the old pine. It was scarred from wind and lightening but it had survived every challenge that came along. Even when strong winds snapped off the younger pines, this old pine barely lost a needle. Amazingly, what finally destroyed this grand old pine tree was not a storm; it was a heavy snow that piled up on its branches. No one would be able to say which snowflake was the proverbial "last straw" that accomplished what years of storms had been unable to do, but the weight of many tiny snowflakes snapped off the old tree's magnificent and full crown.

The article where I read this parable was talking about debt. Most of us know that debt is something that can slowly–but–significantly erode one's economic ability to recover. One little thing can tip the scales from a person's carrying a lot of debt to becoming bankrupt.

However, I thought the parable was equally true of how sin can destroy us. Sin is a reality for all of us. St. John says at the beginning of his letter: "if we say, 'we are without sin,' we deceive ourselves." We confess as we begin each Mass that we are sinners and ask for God's mercy. Like tiny, innocuous looking snowflakes, sin can have a way of creeping up on us. We tell ourselves things like "oh, that's not so bad," or "everybody's doing it," or "God is forgiving," or "no one will know," "nobody's perfect," or whatever. For the most part, each of these statements can be absolutely true: it's not so bad, everybody's doing it, God is forgiving, no one will know, nobody's perfect but like little snowflakes that keep falling, we don't notice how certain habits can grow. St. John tells us in today's second reading "I am writing this to you so that you may not commit sin." Before I move in a more positive direction with what I have to say about sin, I would like to insert what I believe is the most dangerous sin our culture has to deal with today – ignoring the Third Commandment, to keep holy the Lord's Day. To too many people it doesn't seem to be a big deal, yet it denies God the honor due to God and it breaks one's connection with the body of Christ, the community of believers, which gives us spiritual nourishment and guidance.

St. John has more to say about sin than to tell us we're all guilty. He goes on to say, "if anyone does sin, we have an Advocate with the Father, Jesus Christ the righteous one." Our readings at this time of the year proclaim the resurrection, but they also continuously call us to live the new life Christ came to bring us and to turn away from whatever interferes with our relationship with our risen Lord. Did you notice how in last Sunday's gospel, the first thing Jesus said to the apostles after greeting them with "Peace be with you," he said "Receive the Holy Spirit, whose sins you forgive they are forgiven them"? In our first reading, Peter calls his listeners to repent and be converted that their sins may be wiped away. In today's gospel, Jesus tells his apostles, "Thus it is written that the Christ would suffer and rise from the dead on the third day and that repentance, for the forgiveness of sins, would be preached in his name to all the nations."

Dr. Karl Menninger, a well-known psychiatrist, wrote a very perceptive book entitled Whatever Became of Sin. He ends his book by saying the first thing we have to do to change anything about ourselves that perhaps we should change is to face it. Last Sunday is often designated as Diving Mercy Sunday. I'm all for Divine Mercy and I'm grateful that God's mercy is available any time we turn to him and ask his forgiveness. I suppose it's called Divine Mercy Sunday because of last week's gospel, but today has every right to be called Divine Mercy Sunday. Truly, on every Sunday, or every time we come to Mass, we begin asking for God's mercy. We say in the Our Father, "forgive us our trespasses;" we say before Communion, "Lord I am not worthy."

I suppose if a person is burdened with guilt, Divine Mercy Sunday would be a good reminder that God is merciful and forgives us when we turn back to him, but we must always know God is kind and merciful. It's the way he identified himself to Moses (Exodus 34:6), the way he identified himself throughout the whole Old Testament, the way he presents himself to us in Jesus, and for that we give thanks.

Fourth Sunday of Easter
April 29, 2012

INTRODUCTION – (*Acts 4:8-12; 1 John 3:1-2; John 10:11-18*) Last week in my introduction to the first reading from the Acts of the Apostles I spoke about how Peter and John healed a crippled beggar in the Temple. The healed man jumped up and down and was walking around which caused a great amount of commotion in the Temple. Those who were in the Temple at the time wanted to know what happened and how it had happened. Peter's speech on that occasion was the first reading last week. Peter gave all the credit to the risen Jesus who had healed the man through the Apostles. Many of the Jewish religious leaders did not believe in the possibility of a resurrection. When they heard what was going on, they arrested Peter and John. They didn't want to hear any more about Jesus who was a threat to their position. Today we hear a portion of Peter's testimony before the Jewish court. Notice not only what Peter had to say about Jesus but also his boldness. The court didn't know what to do with Peter and John for all the people in Jerusalem were excited and happy about the healing of the man who had been lame for over 40 years. So the court officials warned the Apostles not to talk about Jesus any more. The Apostles were not intimidated for they were now filled with the Holy Spirit. (*Acts 4:8-12*)

HOMILY – Two ladies from New York had always lived a pretty sheltered life. One day they decided to take a trip to England. While they were touring the countryside, the one said to the other: "Look at those white cows. I've never seen cows like that before." The other replied: "Maybe they are albino. Or perhaps a special British type of cow." The guy sitting behind them said: "Those cows are sheep." Sheep are not as common a sight in the U.S. as they are in other countries – especially in the Middle East. On a trip several years ago, we saw a lot of sheep in Israel. Once or twice our tour bus had to stop for about five minutes or so as a very large flock of sheep crossed the road with their shepherd.

I know I've mentioned this before, but it was one of the most beautiful sights was as I was coming down Mt. Sinai. It took, I think, about eight hours to climb up and as we were coming down we saw a shepherdess with her little flock of sheep scattered on a nearby mountain trying to find bits and pieces of vegetation on the barren rocks. As we watched this peaceful scene as the sun was going down, she got out her shepherds' flute and started walking toward wherever she lived. As she played a little tune, the sheep all fell into line and followed her until they rounded a bend and were out of sight. Jesus says of the shepherd: "he walks ahead of them, and the sheep follow him." (*Jn 10:4*) Because sheep were a major part of Jewish life, culture and economy, Jesus' listeners could relate to what Jesus preached a lot more easily than we can.

What Jesus said about shepherds we would understand better by making comparisons with dedicated parents or security personnel such as the firemen and policemen and women who sacrificed their lives on 9/11 to save others.

One thing that will help us understand Jesus' parable of the good shepherd is to look back in the Old Testament to the Book of Ezekiel. God condemned the kings and priests at the time of the prophet Ezekiel (almost 600 years before Christ), because they were leading people away from God and not closer to God – which they should have done. Ezekiel compared the Jewish leaders to shepherds who had no concern for the sheep, the people, but they used the people only to enrich themselves. Ezekiel tells these wicked leaders: "Thus says the Lord God: I myself will look after and tend my sheep. In good pastures will I pasture them. I will give them rest, the lost I will seek out, the strayed I will bring back, the injured I will bind up, the sick I will heal shepherding them rightly." (*Ezekiel 34:11*)

Jesus is the fulfillment of Ezekiel's prophecy. He continues to guide us to eternal life, if we will follow him. We have all gone through those times when we don't know where he's taking us, perhaps many times. That's why he tells us to trust him.

I am reminded of a little story. A holy man took a trip to a town with which he was unfamiliar. He took with him a lamp, a rooster and a donkey. When he could not find a place to stay in the town, he went into the nearby woods to sleep. He lit his lamp to read the Scriptures, but a strong wind blew the lamp over and it broke. So he said, "all that God does, he does well" and fell asleep. During the night, wild animals chased away the rooster and thieves stole the donkey. When he woke as the sun came up, they were gone, yet the holy man said, "all that God does, he does well." He then went back into the village to see if any rooms where he could stay had become available. When he got there he discovered enemy soldiers had been there during the night and killed everyone in the town. He also learned these enemy soldiers had traveled through the part of the woods where he was sleeping. Had his lamp not been broken, he would have been discovered. Had not the rooster been chased, it would have crowed, giving him away. Had not he donkey been stolen, it would have brayed. So once more the holy man declared: "All that God does, he does well." We just have to be careful not to say that every bad thing that happens is God's doing. People do bad things against God's wise plan or against God's laws out of ignorance or evil or for whatever reason. We have to remember what Paul said: "for those who love God, everything works out for the best." Amen.

Fifth Sunday of Easter
May 3, 2015

INTRODUCTION – (*Acts 9, 26-31; I John 3, 18-24;*

John 15, 1-8) Our first reading from the Acts of the Apostles is about St. Paul whose Jewish name was Saul. Here he is called by his Jewish name. Paul was a zealous Pharisee and a fierce persecutor of all who believed in Christ. He was most likely one of the leaders of the crowd who killed Stephen, the first Christian martyr. Once, as he was on his way to Damascus to search out Christians and arrest them, Jesus appeared to him. In an instant Paul realized Christians had it right and he was 100 percent wrong. His life turned around completely and he began preaching and teaching about Jesus - that he was Savior and Messiah. Even after Paul preached about Jesus for three years, the Christian community in Jerusalem was not convinced that he could be trusted. When he first showed up in Jerusalem, after his conversion (which is what we hear about in today's first reading), the disciples were afraid of him. The disciples did put complete faith in a disciple named Barnabas who testified that Paul's faith in Jesus was genuine. Thus, through Barnabas, Paul was welcomed into the community. However, there were a group of Jews who spoke Greek called the Hellenists. They refused to accept Paul because of his faith in Jesus and they saw him as a traitor to Judaism. For his own safety, Paul had to leave Jerusalem. He headed back to his hometown of Tarsus in modern day Turkey. He lived there for maybe three or four years before he began his famous missionary journeys which take up the final two-thirds of the Acts of the Apostles.

HOMILY – "I am the vine, you are the branches." Throughout John's gospel, Jesus is trying to reveal himself to us. In order to help us know him, Jesus uses the words "I Am" quite often. Sometimes he uses "I am" without a predicate such as when he said "Amen, Amen, I say to you, before Abraham came to be, I am." (*Jn. 8,*

58) Other times Jesus uses images to describe himself such as: "I am the light of the world," (Jn. 9, 5) or "I am the resurrection and the life," (Jn. 11, 25) or "I am the good shepherd," (Jn. 10,11) or "I am the bread of life," (Jn. 6, 35), "I am the way, the truth and the life" (Jn. 14,6) or as we hear today: "I am the vine, you are the branches," (Jn. 15, 5).

To understand this image, we need to picture a vine in our minds. Most probably Jesus had in mind a grape vine as they are common all over the world. They are made up of a stem or stalk that is rooted in the ground and they contain many branches. The grapes grow on the branches. That is the whole vine. When Jesus says I am the vine, he is envisioning this entire plant. When he says you are the branches, he is telling us we are part of him; his life flows into us producing leaves and fruit and the fruit we produce is his love in us that flows out of us in the good works we do. It is an image that demonstrates the greatest possible union that we have with Jesus.

It's very similar to the image St. Paul uses in his first letter to the Corinthians when he tells us in Chapter 12 that we are the body of Christ. Just like the body is made up of many parts: hands, feet, heart, lungs, arms, legs, Christ is made up of many members, but we are all one in Christ. This unity is established through believing in Jesus, hearing his word and following his teachings, and in a special way through the Eucharist. It is in the Eucharist that he feeds and nourishes us, just like the roots of the vine pull nourishment out of the ground and nourish the vine or like a hamburger sandwich which we eat nourishes all the parts of our body.

Jesus, who tells us "I am the bread of life," nourishes us with his word and with his own body and blood. I know myself, when my schedule gets really wild, and I don't get to spend some quiet time in church, I really feel the emptiness and chaos in my life and I have to get back here in church and spend some quiet time to get strength and peace again.

So our gospel focuses on three main actors: we have the Father who is the vine grower, Jesus who is the vine, and we who are the branches connected to and part of the vine. The Father who cares for the vine helps us and encourages us to produce more good works so God's love can show itself in a greater and greater way in the world. May God's life and love grow in us and may we always stay united with Jesus the vine through the bread of life he offers us each weekend. Amen.

Sixth Sunday of Easter
May 10, 2015

INTRODUCTION – Two thousand years ago, as the message of Jesus started to spread, a major issue arose in the early Church. Jesus was a Jew, the Apostles were Jews, and Jesus' first followers were Jews. The issue was: what about Gentiles who were pagans? When they became believers and followers of Jesus, should they be circumcised, and follow Jewish dietary laws, and celebrate on Jewish feasts, and offer sacrifices in the Temple as prescribed in the Torah. (*Acts 10, 25-26,34-35,44- 48*)

St. Peter, the leader of the community of those who believed in Jesus, received the answer to this question in a very unusual way. While in prayer, God gave Peter a vision of many different birds and animals. Many of them were birds and animals the Jews were not allowed to eat, such as pork, shrimp, clams, oysters and many other creatures. (*Lev. 11,1-23*) God told Peter to eat them. Peter said he would never eat any food that the Law regarded as unclean. God said to him: "What God has made clean, you are not to call unclean." God repeated this three times to Peter. Then when the vision disappeared, God told Peter there were some men coming to see him and he was to go with them to the home of a Gentile named Cornelius, a high officer in the Roman army. A strict Jew was not allowed to enter a Gentile's house, but God told him to, so Peter did. Cornelius had a gathering of many relatives and friends (all pagan) at his home waiting for Peter. Cornelius told Peter an angel had appeared to him and told him to send for Peter. So Peter spoke to the group about Jesus. Almost Peter's entire speech has been left out of our reading, but you can look it up in your Bibles when you get home. Today's liturgy wants to focus on the response of the pagan Gentiles, how the Holy Spirit came upon them and how Peter baptized them without insisting that they first convert to Judaism before accepting Jesus into their lives. This gave Peter the answer as to how the Apostles were to deal with Gentiles who wanted to convert to Christ.

HOMILY – (*2nd Reading: 1 John: 4,7-10; Gospel: John 15,9-17*) Happy mothers' day to all our mothers, grandmothers, step-mothers and others who offer motherly support in a loving way. Charles Dickens, taking a line from the book of Exodus, wrote about God visiting punishment on the next generation for the sins of their fathers. Dickens asked why God didn't say something about the blessings that God sent on the next generation for the virtues of their mothers. A good point! An overworked mother wrote into a newspaper that the quickest way for a mother to get her children's attention is to sit down and look comfortable. A Jewish proverb says "God could not be everywhere, and therefore he created mothers." (*various items from Holy Humor, by Cal and Rose Samra, pg 81-85*).

Love is in our minds and hearts today as we recall the love of our parents, specifically the love and dedication of our mothers. Love is also in the readings for today. Our first reading tells us of God's love as God reveals his love and salvation to people of every race and culture in the conversation of the Roman officer with his family and friends. John's letter, our second reading, tells us everyone who loves is begotten by God and knows God. In today's gospel, as Jesus gathers with his disciples at the Last Supper, he focuses his remarks on love. He had just told them, as we heard last week: "I am the vine, you are the branches. Remain in me, as I remain in you." The image of vine and branches symbolized the intimate sharing of life and love that we can have with him if we choose to remain in him.

I have spoken of love many times especially of the three words the Greeks had to describe love: agape, philia and eros. Eros you can figure out from the English word "erotic." Philia gave a name to one of our major cities, Philadelphia, which is called the city of brotherly love. Philia means friendship love. Whereas Philia refers to a kind of mutuality, two people benefitting from the relationship they have with each other, agape refers to an unselfish kind of love, a giving kind of love in which a person does not ask anything in return. God's love is agape. God's love is pure gift. We don't make God any richer or happier or greater than he already is when we love him, but when we love him, it is we who benefit, who are richer, happier and greater than we would be without him. God is always the giver – that's why we so often use the word "grace" in our theology because "grace" means gift.

Whenever we hear Jesus speak the word "love" in our

reading today, in the original Greek version of the gospel, the word used was agape. He wants our love to be like his. "This is my commandment, love one another as I love you." How do we manage to have that kind of unselfish love, a love that is willing to lay down one's life for another? We can only have agape love with help from the source of all love, God who is love.

Jesus tells us we will be greatly blessed if we do what he tells us to do and if we keep his commandment (he calls it a commandment because we don't always feel like being loving people). Our blessings will be, first of all, joy: "I told you this so that my joy may be in you." We will know Christ's friendship, we will be chosen to bear good fruit (i.e. we will do good works) and God will hear our prayers and answer them: "whatever you ask the Father in my name he will give you." Does that give us enough reason to try to face each day and the people we meet (even our enemies) with agape love? Happy Mothers' day to all the mothers who have loved their families with this kind of unselfish, devoted love. Amen.

Feast of the Ascension
May 17, 2015

HOMILY – (*Acts 1:1-11; Ephesians 1:17-23: Mark 16:15-20*) If you think of the Ascension of Jesus as a historical event, you will be very confused if you try to figure out just where it took place and when. Matthew does not tell us when Jesus ascended, but he does tell us he ascended from Galilee. John seems to tell us that the ascension occurred most probably before Jesus appeared to the Apostles on Easter Sunday night. Luke tells us in his gospel that Jesus ascended from Bethany on Easter Sunday night, but in his second book, the Acts of the

Apostles, he tells us Jesus ascended from the mount called Olivet (pretty much the same as Bethany) 40 days after Easter.

Mark's gospel, which we have just heard briefly, tells of some of the appearances of Jesus found in Luke and John's gospels. Mark's gospel focuses on faith and baptism and the healing powers Jesus gave to the apostles. It does not tell us when the ascension took place. Today's gospel describes the heavenly glory to which Jesus has returned as he directs the Apostles to preach the gospel to the whole world.

So you see, it's hard to pin down the time and place of the ascension. It's easier to think of it as a process rather than a historical moment. The process of ascending to the Father initially put an end to the visible activity of Jesus here on earth, except for those special times when Jesus appeared to someone. His human body, which he took on through the incarnation, would **now** be with his disciples in a spiritual way - while at the same time he would be gloriously enthroned at the right hand of God the Father. But for a period of time, perhaps in round numbers it was about 40 days, Jesus appeared often in order to strengthen the faith of the Apostles and to prepare them to witness to his life, death and resurrection to the ends of the earth.

There are many lessons we can draw from the ascension of Jesus. There is a passage in John's gospel that is especially meaningful to me. It does not specifically describe the ascension of Jesus, but the ascension of Jesus is implied. It was said at the Last Supper by Jesus who was trying to help his disciples deal with the trauma they would soon be experiencing when Jesus would be arrested, tortured and crucified. Jesus said to them: "Do not let your hearts be troubled" (a big order with all that would soon happen). Jesus continued "you have faith in God; have faith also in me. In my Father's house there are many dwelling places. If there were not, would I have told you that I am going to prepare a place for you? And if I go and prepare a place for you I will come back again and take you to myself, so that where I am you also may be." (Jn. 14,1-3) These few verses presuppose the ascension and I find them most comforting. There **is** another world Jesus wants to make us a part of; a world where his glory and love will be fully revealed and experienced. Thomas asked the question: where is that world and how do we get there? Jesus told him that world will be found by following Jesus, for he said, "I am the way and the truth and the life. No one comes to the Father except through me." (Jn. 14,6) Amen.

For those who celebrated the feast of the Ascension on Thursday, here is the Mass for the Seventh Sunday of Easter.

Seventh Sunday of Easter
May 16, 1999

HOMILY – *(Acts 1:15-17, 20-26, 1 John 4:11-15, John 17:11-19)* Jesus was asked one time what is the most important commandment in the law. We know how he answered. He not only gave us the most important commandment but the second most important commandment as well, two commands that perfectly compliment each other: to love God with our whole heart and soul and mind and strength and to love our neighbor as ourselves. Jesus gave us the answer not only by his words but also by the way he lived.

I would like to reflect today on how Jesus showed love

for his Father. His perfect obedience was one way he showed his love. Another way he showed it was by spending time with his Father in prayer. That is what we especially want to focus on today. The topic of prayer was inspired by today's gospel which is part of Jesus prayer at the Last Supper. We have little or no information about what his life was like before he began his public ministry. The little information we do have shows us that Joseph and Mary were faithful in their Jewish observances. Thus Jesus would have been brought up in that tradition, going to synagogue on the Sabbath and going to the Temple in Jerusalem annually for Passover. St. Luke tells us that when Jesus was beginning his ministry he went to Nazareth and went to the synagogue on the Sabbath "according to his custom."

Synagogue services would have been very similar to the first part of our Mass. There would be common prayer and readings from the Law and the prophets and with a commentary after each reading. St. Luke points out in his gospel that Jesus was praying as John the Baptist baptized him. Immediately after that, recall how Jesus went into the desert for 40 days to fast and pray. His encounter with the devil there showed he knew the scriptures well and he could quote them easily. Frequently it is mentioned that during his public ministry Jesus was at the Temple participating in liturgical celebrations there. The gospels tell us about Jesus getting up early in the morning to pray or staying up all night in prayer. He would spend time in prayer before important decisions or important events. One time after seeing Jesus praying, the disciples asked him to teach them to pray and of course we are all familiar with the prayer he taught them. In addition to the Our Father, Jesus taught a lot about prayer. For example the parable of a man who had a friend visit him at night and he went to his neighbor to borrow some food, and he kept on knocking until he got what he needed. That's the way Jesus said we should pray. Even when he wasn't teaching about prayer, his teachings reflect the deep relationship Jesus had with his Father. There is no doubt about it, prayer played a major role in Jesus' life. The Last Supper of course was more than an ordinary supper. It was the Passover which Jesus was celebrating with his disciples, which was a religious celebration.

His prayer (in the 17th chapter of John) is divided into three parts. First Jesus prays for himself, then for his apostles, then for all who would come to believe in him. Notice how many times the word "glory" is used in today's gospel. Jesus saw his death and resurrection as a moment of glory, a moment when God's saving love would be revealed to the world. He prays that the Father might be glorified in all that was to take place and that in the fulfillment of his mission, he might be a source of life for all who would believe in him. It is comforting to know he prayed for all of us at the Last Supper. He continues to intercede for us each time we celebrate the Lord's Supper.

There is not the time to analyze this prayer thoroughly. My main point today was simply to point out the prayerfulness of Jesus. We see in the first reading how Jesus followers imitated his example as they gathered together in prayer in the upper room after the Ascension, waiting for the coming of the Holy Spirit. Louis Evely in his book, Teach us to Pray, wrote: "Too many Christians regard God as pilots regard their parachute, namely, good if needed, but better if they can get along without it." We might wonder why would Jesus need to pray? He was already as close to the Father as he possibly could be. I am sure there are many reasons why Jesus prayed, but this question might best be answered with another question: "why do we need to spend time with those who are important to us, with those whom we love?"

A true disciple of our Lord will make prayer a priority in their lives, and by "prayer" I mean more than just a rapidly recited Our Father or Hail Mary. Prayer is spending time with our God. Do we feel like we're too busy? I will never forget what our spiritual director in the seminary told us. The busier we are the more we need to pray.

Today we come together for the greatest prayer there is. As we gather in prayer today, we are not alone and I don't mean simply that there are others here in church with us. Christ is with us and it is in union with his perfect sacrifice of love and obedience on the cross that we offer our prayers and praise to God our Father.

Pentecost
May 24, 2015

INTRODUCTION – We hear in our first reading St. Luke's account in the Acts of the Apostles of the coming of the Holy Spirit on Pentecost. The Spirit came with a loud noise, tongues of fire, and the gift of the apostles being able to speak new languages. The coming of the Holy Spirit took place in the presence of Jews from all over the world. However, the greatest sign of God's Spirit at work was the courage shown in the apostles, especially Peter who just weeks prior was afraid to admit that he even knew Jesus Christ. After the Spirit came, his fear was gone and he went out publicly preaching about him.

HOMILY – Pentecost is one of the oldest and one of the three most important feasts of the Jewish people. In Greek it means 50th day – that is 50 days from Passover. Passover celebrated God freeing his people from their

slavery in Egypt. About a month and a half after leaving
Egypt, God's people arrived at Mt. Sinai where God
made a covenant with his people identifying them as his
special people. The Ten Commandments God gave
them was part of that covenant. Pentecost was a day of
pilgrimage when pious Jews would travel to Jerusalem to
celebrate this event. Jesus' followers were there, 50 days
after Jesus' resurrection. On that occasion, we are told
the Spirit came with a loud noise – like a strong wind –
and in tongues of fire, symbols recalling the way God was
experienced on Mt. Sinai hundreds of years earlier. Also
the Apostles received a unique gift of tongues to be able
to speak in foreign languages. Since Jerusalem was filled
with pilgrims at this time, the Apostles knew what they
were supposed to do with this unusual gift - to tell
anyone around, no matter from what distant place they
came, the good news about Jesus Christ.

A person can hardly talk about Pentecost without
talking about the Holy Spirit. But that opens up a very
large topic. I pulled out my book on the Holy Spirit,
almost 600 pages long, to help me decide what to say.
Even though there's much that could be said, we still
struggle when we try to think about what the Holy Spirit
might be like, might look like, or to try to make contact
with the Spirit. We are taught the Holy Spirit is God,
the third person of the Holy Trinity. The Holy Spirit
will help us if we happen to have to take a test. Pretty
much this is all the typical Catholic knows about the
Holy Spirit and I'll bet the normal Catholic is greatly
surprised to discover that someone could have written a
600-page book all about the Holy Spirit. Let me just
mention some of the symbols of the Holy Spirit that are
mentioned in the Scriptures. The first one is breath, air
or wind. Jesus breathed on them and said "receive the
Holy Spirit." Jesus' breath imparted the Spirit. Water is

another symbol. Jesus said: "let anyone who thirsts come to me and drink. Whoever believes in me, as scripture says. Rivers of living water will flow from within him." He said this in reference to the Spirit. (*Jn 7,37-39*) Fire has been a symbol of God since the days of Moses and the burning bush. That's why red is the color of the Holy Spirit. A dove is a familiar image, but trying to explain the symbolism of a dove would take a few more paragraphs, so we won't go there. Less familiar is the anointing by the Spirit which Jesus talks about using a quote from Isaish: "the Spirit of the Lord is upon me, because he has anointed me." (*Lk, 4,18*) The finger of God is another symbol. It is by the finger of God, the symbol of God's power, that Jesus casts out demons (*Lk 11,20*). There are other names and symbols of the Spirit, such as Paraclete, which would take more time to explain than we have right now. The last symbol I would like to consider is the symbol of the Spirit being a gift from the Father and the Son. Although Jesus is God's gift to us, it is the Spirit who is mostly referred to as a gift (*Acts 8,20; Jn 4,10 & 4,14; Acts 2,38, 10,45 and 11,17 Heb 6,4-6*) My favorite reference to the Spirit as a gift: "what father among you would hand his son a snake when he asks for a fish: Or hand him a scorpion when he asks for an egg? If you then, who are wicked, know how to give good gifts to your children, how much more will the Father in heaven give the Holy Spirit to those who ask him?" (*Lk.11,12*) I am grateful that God is so lavish with God's gift of the Spirit, but if I put them all together, I still struggle, in spite of all the symbols the Scriptures use, to relate to the Spirit, to connect with the Spirit, to know the Spirit as a person.

A thought came to me this week that helped me picture the Spirit a little more concretely. Look into your own heart or look into a mirror. St. Paul asks: "Do you not know that you are the temple of God and that the Spirit of God dwells in you." (*I Cor 3,16*) I'm not saying every simple detail you see in yourself is of God. It may not be. Paul lists a whole batch of human traits that are not of God: "idolatry, hatred, rivalry, jealousy, outbursts of fury, selfishness, envy, etc." Paul also gives us a long list of traits that are from God: love, joy, peace, patience, kindness, generosity, faithfulness, gentleness, self-control." (*Gal, 5,19-24*) Do you see these traits in yourselves, do you see them in others, then you are seeing what the Holy Spirit looks like.

We should see these traits in the Church too, for the Holy Spirit, as we just heard, gave life to the Church at Pentecost by sending the Apostles out to proclaim the gospel of Jesus Christ. Without Pentecost, the Church would have died a quick death because the Apostles were too afraid to proclaim Jesus Christ. But with the Spirit, the Church came alive. That's why we call Pentecost the birthday of the Church. It is through grace and the Sacraments, the Spirit continues to work to help the Church to grow. Take a look at yourself in the mirror sometime this evening or take a look at a friend whom you love and who believes in God as you do and say to yourself "that's what the Spirit looks like when we hold God in our hearts." Amen.

Feast of the Holy Trinity
May 31, 2015

INTRODUCTION – (*Deuteronomy 4,32-34.39-40; Romans 8,14-17; Matthew 28,16-20*) This is the time for commencement addresses as people graduate and move on in life. Today's first reading is like a commencement address Moses is giving to God's people as they prepare to enter the Promised Land.

Moses knew he had to part from the people for he was soon to die. So he shares some words of wisdom with the people before they crossed the Jordan into the Land that would be their new home. He tells them there is no other God than the Lord (Yahweh) and that only by being faithful to their God will they prosper. His advice is good advice for today's world where polytheism and paganism, which were popular in the days of Moses, have been replaced by atheism, hedonism and materialism.

HOMILY – Today's feast traces its origin back to the fourth century during the time of the Arian heresy. Arianism taught that Jesus was not fully God. It taught that he was a creature higher than the angels but not equal to God the Father. The heresy almost destroyed the Church. The Council of Nicea (in 325 A.D.) proclaimed that Jesus was equal to the Father in every way and we profess that as our faith every week in the Nicene Creed. Indeed it is a great mystery how God is three persons, the Father, the Son and the Holy Spirit. These three persons are so closely united in nature and in love that we proclaim there is only one God. This mystery is revealed to us in the Scriptures and it helps us understand the Scriptures better, but it remains a mystery and will always be a mystery until we are fully united with the Trinity in heaven. There is one important element that can help us understand the Trinity just a little bit more, and that is love. In everyday experience we have seen that love has the power to draw two people together and make them one in mind and heart and yet the two people retain their individuality. The Bible tells us God is love, and it is the power of divine love that makes Father, Son and Holy Spirit one God without destroying the distinction between the three persons. It is that love that overflowed and created the universe. It is that love that made us, redeemed us and has forgiven our sins and that calls us to enjoy eternal bliss in the kingdom of heaven when it comes time for us to leave this world.

Now I need to change the subject. (volunteers start passing out "Dedication Weekend" cards.) About three months ago I spoke about a major campaign in the Archdiocese that all parishes would participate in called One Faith, One Hope, One Love. We have not had a campaign like this since 1955 when I graduated from High School. The campaign in '55 was meant primarily to build Catholic High Schools. This current campaign is meant to give financial aid to parents who want to get their children into a Catholic school but who cannot afford the full tuition. One Faith, One Hope, One Love will also be used to help the poor though Catholic Social Services; it will help support priests in their retirement (with priests living longer and with fewer younger priests the retirement fund is greatly underfunded); it will help promote vocations; and 20% of what we raise will come back to St. Boniface to be used for whatever projects we might have. We thought increasing parking close to Church would be a worthwhile project.

Today is meant to wrap up all our efforts to reach our goal. We could make it in the next couple of weeks. We have gifts and pledges of about $500,000 which means we are about $70,000 short of our goal. I have been so impressed with the generosity of our parishioners. I thank you. And I thank Rick Salerno and his group of volunteers for all their work throughout these past six months. What we want to do today is to be sure everyone has been contacted. You should have received a card like this.

Before I describe the card I want you to fill out, I want to say this: a kind person I know has offered $40,000 as a matching gift to help us reach our goal. If we get pledges today, or any increases, up to $40,000, my friend will match it. So if you give $500 dollars it will be like you just gave $1000.

Please print your name, address, etc. on the card. (this will help keep our census up to date too). On that same side of the card, there are four options and I would ask if you would check one: 1) that you are making a pledge today, 2) that you have already made a pledge, 3) that you are still thinking about it, or 4) that you cannot participate at this time. If you have said "no" we will not try to twist your arm.

If you checked that you will make a pledge today, just fill in the blanks at the bottom of the card. If you are still making up your mind, we will try to get back to you. It would be a great favor to us if you check off something, so we know we contacted you and we won't keep trying to reach you.

I will give you a couple of minutes to fill out the card, then fold them in half and the ushers will collect them. After the cards are collected, we will have our regular offertory collection. Thank you for your patience and again I thank every person who has had some part in helping us attain the level of success we have achieved.

The Body and Blood of Christ
June 7, 2015

INTRODUCTION – (*Exodus 24: 3-8; Hebrews 9: 11-15; Mark 14: 12-16,22-26*) Our first reading brings us into the desert of Sinai, about 1300 years before Christ. There we meet Moses in charge of a motley bunch of Hebrews, leading them from their slave master in Egypt (who was probably Ramses II) to a new land they could call their own. We hear how God made a covenant with this bunch of people, a solemn pact by which he promised they would be his special people and they promised they would follow the law he gave them. I can't stress enough how important this passage is. Every detail deserves attention, but today's liturgy is especially interested in focusing on the theme of blood. It was often the custom in those days to use blood to ratify or to make a covenant binding. So Moses took the blood of sacrificed animals and sprinkled half of it on an altar which was used to represent God and he sprinkled half of it on the people. God and the people were thus bound together in a most solemn and serious bond. This covenant defined the Jews for centuries and much of the rest of the Bible pretty much describes the history of how God's people either observed or failed to observe this covenant and the consequences that resulted from their fidelity or infidelity. From their daily prayers to their most solemn feasts, the Jewish people always reflected on their covenant with the God who made them his special people.

One such solemn feast was the feast of Yom Kippur. It was the only day of the year that the high priest could enter the Holy of Holies where the Arc of the Covenant was kept. He approached the Arc of the Covenant with the blood of sacrificial animals, and he sprinkled it on the top of the Arc (called the mercy seat) asking God to forgive the sins of God's people. The blood symbolized the lives of God's people offering themselves to God asking for his mercy. Our second reading refers to this event. Assuming the reader knew all about this ritual, the Letter to the Hebrews tells us how Jesus, our high priest of the new covenant, entered into the eternal sanctuary, the highest heaven, the abode of God. Jesus entered with his own blood which he shed for us for the forgiveness of sins to make an eternal and perfect sacrifice to the Father.

HOMILY – For how many centuries did human beings think the earth was flat and that the sun and moon and stars revolved around this flat earth? People thought that's the way it was because that's the way it looked. There are people who use this same logic when it comes to the Eucharist. "How can this man give us his flesh to eat?" people asked when Jesus told them he was the bread of life. (Jn. 6,52) Jesus said many things that showed he spoke with authority and power: he healed the sick, raised the dead and calmed the storm, but he also said many things that had to be taken on faith, such as: "your sins are forgiven," or that he was sent by God, or when he said at the Last Supper: "this is my body," and "this is my blood." When we hear those words from Jesus we have to think: "Do I believe that?" It's a question that gives rise to another question: "do I believe Jesus, or do I need to see proof?" There were those during Jesus' time who believed Jesus even though they didn't understand, and there were those who could not be convinced no matter how many miracles they saw.

Our feast of the Body and Blood of Christ (Corpus Christi) is meant to strengthen our faith in the real presence of Jesus in the Eucharist. In Matthew, Mark, Luke, I Corinthians and especially in John's gospel, Jesus is most clear in telling us that the Eucharist is truly his body and blood. Yet, many people try to explain away these very direct words of Jesus "this is my body" and "this is my blood" because they cannot see it. They forget the words of Jesus to Thomas: "blessed are those who have not seen and have believed." (Jn.20,29) I know you believe or you wouldn't be here. I am sure you desire to strengthen that belief and I hope that our prayers today will deepen that belief.

I would like to reflect on some of the other things Jesus told us in today's gospel. In receiving Jesus in Communion, we are not only being united with him, we are renewing his covenant with us. "This is the blood of the covenant" he tells us. In this covenant, promises are made. He promises us his eternal love and everlasting life and we promise to live as he has taught us. Do we always live up to that promise? We know we don't, and Jesus knows it also. That's why Jesus gave the apostles the power to forgive sins. That's why we begin Mass asking forgiveness for our sins. In most expressions of the words over the cup, Jesus refers to his blood which is poured out for many. Jesus' death was poured out for us. "Many" in Hebrew or Aramaic can be understood here in the sense of "all." In Matthew's gospel, Jesus said his blood is poured out for many for the forgiveness of sins. His Eucharist, like his death, is a sacrifice. Sometimes we forget why we are here. We sometimes think the Mass is all about us, it should make us feel good or feel holy or something (and that's great when it does move us deeply and spiritually), but the Mass is also something we are offering to God as an act of worship. It is a perfect sacrifice that we now participate in: Jesus giving himself to the Father for us, we participate in that by giving ourselves to the Father in love. Our covenant with God is solemnly made in the blood of Jesus. Jesus ends today's gospel by saying he would not drink of the fruit of the vine until he drinks it new in the kingdom of God. At Mass we look forward to joining him. Amen.

10th Sunday in Ordinary Time
June 9, 1991
HOMILY – (*Genesis 3:9-15; 2 Corinthians 4:13-5:1; Mark 3:29-35*) Do you ever really feel like being bad?

Even though you know how you will feel afterwards? Even though you know how much trouble you can get into? Even though you know how stupid it might be? We all feel that way from time to time. We call it temptation.

Like Adam and Eve, we like to think it is someone else's fault that we are tempted – Adam blamed Eve; Eve blamed the devil. It is often true someone else might deliberately, or even inadvertently, get us going in the wrong direction. But the desire to do wrong really comes out of our own selves – no one makes us do wrong. No one could really tempt us if we didn't let them, if there wasn't something inside of us that wanted to go along with what the tempter suggests.

This feeling we all experience at times to really be bad seems to be built into our human nature. It is one of the leftover effects we suffer from original sin. If we accept the fact we are this way at times, and if we add to this the fact there is a hostile power of evil roaming through the world called the devil, is it any wonder the world is so troubled?

Our theme today, though, is not to convince us there is evil in the world – that's obvious. It is that Christ has overcome the power of evil. In the first reading, God is saying there will be a constant struggle between the powers of evil and the human race. He says to the serpent, "I will put enmity between you and the woman, between your offspring and hers." He adds that evil will be defeated when he tells the serpent, "He (the offspring of Eve) will strike at your head, while you (the serpent) strike at his heel." The human race will be wounded by evil – as if one's heel is struck a blow, but the powers of evil will be fatally wounded because their head will be struck a blow. This image is often portrayed in the statue of Mary who is standing on a serpent or has the head of a serpent under her heel. It is her son who has struck a fatal blow against the powers of evil. This is seen in the gospel where Jesus was casting out demons.

There is only one way evil can triumph and that is when we deliberately blind ourselves to God's saving work - this is what Jesus calls the sin against the Holy Spirit. The Jewish leaders refused to see the power of God at work in Jesus and said his power came from the devil. God can forgive anything except a refusal to be open to God. Such refusal in itself closes out God's love and grace. It creates a wall God's mercy cannot penetrate. This is why it is an eternal sin.

For those who are open to God, those who do his will, they will be closer to Jesus than if they were blood relatives. "Whoever does the will of God is brother and sister and mother to me." Even when evil sometimes has its way with us, Christ has destroyed its power to fully do us in. With Christ we can always get the upper hand.

11th Sunday in Ordinary Time
June 14, 2015

INTRODUCTION – (*Ezekiel 17:22-24; 2 Corinthians 5:6-10; Mark 4:26-34*) The prophet Ezekiel, who is famous for his vision of the dry bones, speaks to us today about trees. He gives us two images. The first image is that God would take a cutting from a tree and plant it in Israel where it would grow into a majestic tree. The prophecy comes from that time in history when Jerusalem's king and the leading citizens of Israel were captured by the Babylonians and were taken off to Babylon as slaves. To finish the job, the Babylonians executed all the king's sons. This was 400 years after King David and it seemed to be the end of the Davidic monarchy which had lasted for that many years. **But** Ezekiel's image of the tiny cutting from a tree which grew into a majestic tree in Israel told God's people that God would raise up a future king from the house of David. In other words, God was not giving up on Israel or the House of David. Ezekiel's prophecy continues with a second image of big trees becoming little trees and vice versa. God would bring low the high tree and lift high the lowly tree which says God would humble the proud and the mighty (Babylon and Egypt) and would raise up the lowly (i.e. Israel). These are messages of hope to a people in despair and their purpose was to give God's people courage as they patiently waited for God to act on their behalf.

HOMILY – Almost every year I get a Christmas card or two that goes something like this: "he was born and grew up in an obscure village, the child of ordinary people. As a young man he worked with his hands as a laborer and in his early 30's, he became an itinerant preacher. He never wrote a book, never held an office, never married or had a family, nor owned a house. When he was only 33, his enemies accused him of insurrection and had him nailed to a cross. His executioners gambled for his clothing. He was laid in a borrowed grave. After 20 centuries he is the central figure of the human race. All the kings that ever reigned, all the armies that ever marched have not affected the lives of people on earth as much as that one solitary life."

And in **three years** Jesus was able to accomplish all he needed to accomplish to make his impact on the world. Compare this with the Buddha who worked for 45 years, or Moses who was the leader of God's people for 40 years, or Mohammed who published his revelations over a period of 22 years. And to do what Jesus did, he didn't have to travel to or study in any of the great cities of the Roman empire of that time.

Jesus' two parables today about the growth of the seed and the tiny mustard seed indicate Jesus had great confidence in where his ministry was going. Today, the number of those who believe in Christ outnumber every other religion. The largest group of believing Christians are Catholics – there are about 1.2 billion in the world. Second are those who follow Mohammed, including both Sunnis and Shiites. The third largest group are non-believers and close to them are the Hindus. Those who follow the Chinese traditional folk beliefs are next in line followed by the Buddhists. By comparison, the Jews make up hardly one fourth of one percent of the world's population. You didn't need to know all of that, but once I got started looking it up, I found it quite interesting.

I don't want to turn this into an opportunity to pat ourselves on the back as Catholics and say we're the biggest group. We have to be humble enough to know that could quickly change as the culture of today's world seems intent on destroying the traditional values of our faith. Mere numbers are not necessarily impressive, for in the spiritual realm, it is not quantity that counts so much as quality. When we talk about quality, the message of the gospel is brought directly to each one of us personally. Are we growing spiritually? If the parables today are not telling each of us we need to be growing in our faith, then they are not telling us anything. As I was reflecting on this parable, it struck me that Jesus' use of a plant as a symbol of growth was brilliant. Think about this: plants either keep growing or they die. This is not the way it works with animals. When animals reach maturity, whether domesticated or wild, they may grow a little by learning a trick or two if they are taught or if they are very bright, but by and large, when they mature, other than putting on a little weight or losing it, they do not grow in any way, except they grow older and they die. Humans are an exception. We may not grow much physically, but there seems to be no end to the skills and the knowledge we can acquire if we put out mind to it. In all the ways we can learn and grow, there is one way that is more important than any other. We have another life ahead of us and we must prepare for it. That's what Jesus came to teach us. Jesus called it the kingdom of heaven or the kingdom of God. He said in today's gospel, "this is how it is with the kingdom of God." As long as we are receptive to God's Spirit, we won't stop growing. As we grow we are to produce good works (often symbolized as good fruit) and then will come the time for the harvest. Then God will ask us what have you done with the life, the time, the talents and the opportunities I have given to you? Will we continue growing and producing good works until that time or will we just sit back and tell ourselves we know enough about our faith, we went to Catholic schools, we listen to the homily mostly without falling asleep, we even pray sometimes when it's **not** Sunday, so what more do we need to do? We have to keep developing a deeper relationship with God through prayer; we need to keep doing good works; we need to grow in our faith through reading and reflection; we may have some faults we need to work on. The Kingdom of God is our future when God calls us to leave this world. Will the love of God fill our hearts so that we are ready to fully embrace the Kingdom God has prepared for us?

Birth of John the Baptist
June 24, 2012

INTRODUCTION – (*Isaiah 49:1-6; Acts 13:22-26; Luke 1:57-66, 80*) We are familiar with John the Baptist from the readings during Advent. John was the prophet who immediately preceded Jesus and foretold his coming. John's birthday usually falls on a weekday, but it is considered such an important feast that when it falls on Sunday, it takes precedence over the Sunday readings. If you are curious why the feast of his birth is today, consider this. The feast of the Annunciation is celebrated on March 25. When the archangel Gabriel appeared to Mary, the archangel told her that her cousin Elizabeth was already in her sixth month. So add three months to March 25 and we are at June 25. (Since John's birthday is the 24th – he must have come a day early).

The liturgy usually puts the feast day of saints on the day they died and entered into eternal life. But there are only three birthdays. This is because their birth is considered especially holy since they were born free from any sin.

[eve] – Our first reading is from Jeremiah, a prophet who lived 600 years before Christ. As God was telling Jeremiah he was to be a prophet, the reading describes that role. This description of a prophet fits John the Baptist as well.

The gospel is the annunciation to John's father, the old priest Zechariah, that he and his elderly wife would have a child, a special child who would prepare God's people for the coming of the Messiah.

[morning] – In today's first reading, the prophet Second Isaiah, who lived about 500 years before Christ, speaks of some mysterious person who was identified simply as God's servant. This poem and three others in Isaiah's writings are known as Servant Songs. The early Church found these songs described Jesus in a most uncanny way. They are usually read during Holy Week. Today, however, the liturgy applies this second of the Servant Songs to John the Baptist because it states: "the Lord called me from birth, from my mother's womb he gave me my name."

When the archangel Gabriel had appeared to John's father Zachariah nine months earlier, he told him his wife Elizabeth would have a son and he was to be named John. Zachariah and Elizabeth were a very old couple and Zachariah didn't believe the angel. Not smart! He lost the ability to speak because of his lack of faith. (It's like the angel was telling him, "keep your mouth shut and your lack of faith to yourself.") Once Zachariah gave his child the name he had been told to name him, he showed he fully accepted all that the angel told him and his ability to speak returned.

HOMILY – Since I gave a long introduction, I do not have a very long sermon. One of Aesop's most famous fables is the story of the ant and the grasshopper.

The story goes like this: In a field one summer's day, a Grasshopper was hopping about, chirping and singing to its heart's content. An Ant passed by, bearing along with great toil a kernel of corn he was taking to the nest. "Why not come and chat with me," said the Grasshopper, "instead of toiling and moiling in that way?" "I am helping to lay up food for the winter," said the Ant, "and recommend you to do the same." "Why bother about winter?" said the Grasshopper; we have got plenty of food at present." The Ant went on its way and continued its toil. When the winter came, the Grasshopper had no food and found itself dying of hunger, while it saw the ants distributing corn and grain from the stores they had collected in the summer. Then the Grasshopper knew: "It is best to prepare for the days of necessity."

Even 2500 years ago, people knew the importance of preparing for the future. It's still just as true today. If we do not learn this lesson when life is good, we'll learn the hard way when it's too late. This goes for education, investing, health and all kinds of important areas of life. John the Baptist's role in life was to insist on the need to prepare. He called people to repent and prepare for the coming of God's kingdom. His message is as important today as it ever was. There is a kind of new age theology that follows the attitude of the Grasshopper. It says don't worry. Everybody is going to be in heaven in the end (except for someone like Hitler). Although God wants all people to be saved, there are abundant passages in the Scriptures that warn us that we cannot take salvation for granted. Jesus, who came to save us and who revealed to us so clearly the love of God, warned us: "The door to heaven is narrow. Work hard to get in, because many will try to enter and will not be able." (*Luke 13:23*) Jesus' message at the beginning of his ministry was the same message as John the Baptist: "repent and believe in the gospel." The word "believe" means more than saying, "I believe." It means putting our belief into action. Statistics keep coming out that fewer and fewer people are coming to Church, which is an indication that more and more people believe that worship of God is not all that important. I think it's the entitlement mentality. We feel entitled to be happy (even eternally), no matter what we do or how we live. That's not what the Scriptures tell us. I think the most important lesson we can learn from this feast of John the Baptist is to prepare. The fact you are here today is one good sign that you understand we need to prepare to meet our God. Amen.

13th Sunday in Ordinary Time
June 28, 2015

INTRODUCTION – The first reading (*Wisdom 1, 13-15.2.23-24*) tells us God did not make death. Rather, it came about through the envy of the devil. This is obviously a commentary on the story of Adam and Eve in the garden – how they tried to find their happiness and fulfillment by making their own rules rather than doing what God told them to do or not do. They thought God wanted to prevent them from being happy instead of trusting that God had their best interests at heart. The two miracles in today's gospel (*Mark 5, 21-43*) show us what can happen when people really put their trust in Jesus. The second reading is an appeal to the Corinthians (*II Cor. 8,7.9.13-15*) for financial help for the poor in Jerusalem.

HOMILY – This week our Supreme Court was busy making laws that would change many people's lives. I do not want to comment right now on either Supreme Court decision, except to state that even though our government decrees something is legal or illegal, there are laws that speak with higher authority. One such example is that our government considers it perfectly legal and ethical to destroy for any reason the life of an unborn child, while we hold to a higher law that says

"Thou shalt not kill." I'm just a simple parish priest with some knowledge of theology and psychology, but I am not prepared, like some TV news anchors, to come out with a profound statement until I get more information. It's going to take some time for me to digest the ramifications and implications of this week's Supreme Court decisions. I've seen a lot of changes in my 51 years as a priest, changes that have happened very rapidly, and sadly many of these changes conflicted with the morals and values Jesus taught us. Jesus came that we "might have life and might have it to the full." (*John 10,10*) He does not tell us there is any other way than his way. Our gospel today tells us we have a God who is interested in our happiness and our well-being and who through revelation calls us to change our lives so we can find the way to truth and life.

Last Sunday we heard the gospel about Jesus calming a storm on the Sea of Galilee. When he landed in Capernaum, he was immediately approached by the leader of the local synagogue whose 12 year-old daughter was dying. As Jesus was on his way to the house of the synagogue leader to heal her, he was delayed on the way by a woman who had suffered for 12 years with a bleeding problem. We are grateful to Mark for all the detail he gives us about these two miracles, details we don't usually have. He even tells us what was going through the mind of the lady who was constantly losing blood.

One thing we see that these two miracles have in common is the power and importance of faith. He tells the woman her faith has saved her and he tells the father of the 12 year-old girl: "do not be afraid, just have faith." You might wonder, wouldn't it help people's faith if they knew Jesus had raised this little girl back to life, yet he tells the apostles not to tell anyone what he had done. I think this was because the people of that time were not capable of understanding the resurrection yet. They wouldn't understand until after Jesus' own resurrection.

I want to call your attention to several items I think are important in today's gospel. You might notice that one of our stained glass windows depicts this miracle. Jesus healed at least four children that I can immediately think of and it was always the parents who came asking for healing. It is a good reminder to parents of the power and efficacy of intercessory prayer. I want you to notice the sensitivity and tenderness of Jesus. When the woman with the bleeding problem was healed, he knew who did it: the gospel tells us he turned around to see (the Greek says: the woman) who had touched him. He didn't scold her or embarrass her – which he could have done since by Jewish law, she had just made him ritually unclean. Instead he called her "daughter" and he made sure she was perfectly healed as he dismissed her saying: "go in peace and be cured of your affliction." We should notice he took time to talk with her even though he was on an urgent mission. Even if everyone else was nervous about whether he would get to the little girl in time to help her, he knew what he would do. Notice also, after raising the little 12 year old girl, he told her parents to feed her. She would have been weak from her ordeal. One other thing to notice, Jesus never had to appeal to God to work these miracles like we have to do. For example we would have to pray to God asking **God** to make this little girl better. The power of divine life was already in Jesus for he was God Incarnate. All he had to do was say "arise, little girl" and she sat up full of life.

I've not offered the sacrament of the healing of the sick lately for those dealing with sickness or infirmity, even infirmity from old age, so I'll do so after Mass today. If someone you know would like to receive it but who is not here, just catch me next week. Remember, as a sacrament, it is Christ who is touching you, the same Christ who touches you with his love in Holy Communion. Amen

14th Sunday in Ordinary Time
July 5, 2015

INTRODUCTION – (*Ezekiel 2, 2-5; II Cor. 12, 7-10; Mark 6, 1-6*) Sometimes prophets predicted the future, but most of the time their task was to remind God's people of how God wanted them to live. Their efforts were not always appreciated by the people who heard the message. The prophet Ezekiel lived about 600 years before Christ. He had to warn the people of the national disaster that was headed their way if they did not change their ways. In the beginning of his book, he describes, as much as it is possible, a vision of God in heaven. He was so overwhelmed he fell flat onto the ground. This is where our first reading comes in. God got him back on his feet and commissioned him to be a prophet. God cautions Ezekiel that as a prophet he would not have an easy job of it. The passage prepares us for the gospel that tells of Jesus, the greatest prophet of all, who was rejected by his own people when he came to preach in his hometown of Nazareth.

HOMILY – My homily is in two parts: on freedom and on the gospel. This weekend we celebrate our freedom. As we know from history, freedom is not a gift that's simply given to us. It is something we had to work for and even fight for. That's because freedom is something more complex than the simple notion many people have about freedom today. Many of the problems we experience in society today come from a misguided notion of freedom. Too many people think freedom means they should be able to have or do anything they want. This is a recipe for chaos and anarchy. The first thing we need to know about freedom is that in the use of my freedom, I have to be considerate of the freedom of others. For example, I have the right and the freedom to go out for a drive, but so do other people. In my freedom or in my hurry to get somewhere I can't push other people off the road. The irony about freedom is that the more we use freedom to justify serving our own wants and needs, the more we are likely to become a slave to our own basic self-centeredness. We all know people who have allowed freedom to lead them into becoming slaves to their own pride, envy, laziness, lust, avarice, gluttony, and anger, not to mention a variety of other addictions that can enslave us. True freedom requires us to acknowledge our creator who has endowed us with freedom and who has given us a path that will help us maintain that freedom. Or as Jesus said: "If you abide in my word, you are truly my disciples; and you will know the truth, and truth will set you free." Jesus is telling us only freedom that is based on following him (being his disciple) is a freedom that is true. (Jn 8, 31-32) When God led his people out of Egypt, thus releasing them from their cruel slavery, he didn't tell them now you are free, you can go and do whatever you want. He said believe in me, worship me, keep my commandments and then you will prosper. Freedom under God, not freedom from God, is what our hearts truly long for, for our greatest joy and fulfillment is love for God.

Now I would like to shift over to the gospel. When Jesus stepped out of his role as the son of a carpenter and started preaching and working miracles, he shook up a lot of people. He didn't favorably impress the Jewish leaders because their own freedom to do whatever they wanted in interpreting God's law was at stake. He didn't favorably impress the people of his own village of Nazareth, a village of maybe 1600 to 2000 people. I would suspect he and his family were known by everyone. I do not believe he was from a desperately poor family; after all he was a craftsman and a lot of construction was going on in that part of Galilee. To make the argument that the holy family had sufficient resources to support themselves, I can add that the holy family could take time off to go to Jerusalem for Passover every year (*Lk. 2,42*). This means Joseph was not a day laborer; he could afford to take a week or so off every year. However, a craftsman was in a class considerably lower than those who were in the educated class. The people of the village knew this for when he began to teach on the Sabbath they asked: "where did this man get all this? What is this wisdom that has been given to him? What deeds of power are being done by his hands? Is this not the carpenter, the Son of Mary, etc." (*Mk. 6,2- 3*) This same question comes up in John. When the people of Jerusalem hear him teach, they asked: "How did this fellow get his education..." (*Jn 7,15*) His answer was "it comes from him who sent me." (*Jn.7,16*)

You would think that his friends and neighbors in this little village would have been proud of him, but what Jesus was doing was not their tradition. They were slaves to their tradition (remember Tevye in Fiddler on the Roof). Their tradition was like a class system and Jesus was moving into a higher class than that to which he was entitled by birth. The class he was moving into was the educated class. Now, there was no public education system, except for what a child might pick up in the synagogue on the Sabbath. Otherwise it was home schooling for everyone. A girl would learn how to keep house and be a mother while a boy was expected to learn whatever skills his father could teach him so he could support a family. Not only was Jesus stepping out of his class, he was expecting the people of Nazareth to accept his teachings and put their faith in him. Here he was, speaking for God, speaking as a prophet, as one sent by God to teach and to heal, while their previous knowledge of him, the category they had placed him in, kept them from accepting him.

So Jesus speaks the famous line, a line my father loved to say about himself, "prophets are not without honor, except in their hometown, and among their own kin, and in their own house." (*Mk. 6,4*) His own people could not see him as a prophet. We know, however, some of his family later on did end up following him and believing in him. As for my dad. I recognize now I missed out on a lot of wisdom he could have shared with us if I had listened. Sometimes we're too smart for our own good. Let us pray on this day that a distorted sense of freedom does not lead us to think that we're smart enough to ignore the wisdom and the freedom Jesus came to bring us. Amen.

Fr. Lammeier's Funeral
July 11, 2015

HOMILY – (*Isaiah 25:6. 7-9; 1 Thessalonians 4:13-18; John 14:1-6*) I would like to begin with a quotation from Fr. Lammeier's will. No! he did not leave instructions to give everyone $1000 who came to his funeral. But he did give instructions about the homily for his Funeral Mass. He wrote in his will this (quote) "request that the homilist talk on 'death' or the priesthood. Please no eulogy. There is not an awful lot of good that can be said, and I would want the homily to be a little longer than that." (unquote)

I would not agree with Fr. Lammeier on that. There is an "awful lot of good that can be said," but I'm not going to say everything that could be said because I may be haunted by Fr. Lammeier some evening for not following his instructions. I hope no one objects to my calling Fr. Lammeier "Zib." It was a nickname his mother gave him when he was small and he told me he doesn't know what it means or why she called him that. I've been calling him Zib for the past 15 years or more when he was helping me at St. Boniface. We were blest by Fr. Lammeier's willingness to help us. He was a very humble man, highly respected, had a good sense of humor, worked hard on his homilies and described himself as a simple priest who said his prayers and did his work. He influenced many people by his wisdom, whether it was one of the two archbishops he served as their administrative secretary, Archbishops Leibold and Bernardin, or whether it was the ordinary parishioner who came to him with a problem or for confession on a Saturday afternoon. He treated everyone with equal dignity and kindness.

For about 18 months, he lived at St. Boniface Church and it was an honor and privilege to have him there. He tried very hard not to inconvenience any of the staff. Often when people visited him, instead of saying "goodbye" he always said "try to be nice." The way he was telling others to live is the way he lived, treating others in a friendly and benevolent way.

This is getting too much like a eulogy, which Zib didn't want. He said to talk about the priesthood or death. Well, I will say something about both. Regarding priesthood, Zib loved being a priest. Saying Mass in the morning was the highlight of his day. The day he died, he had concelebrated Mass with the other priests at St. Margaret Hall. He was faithful to the divine office, the rosary and holy hours at church. He was not a monk or a hermit, he had a well-rounded personality; he enjoyed reading, watching sports on TV and keeping in touch with his many friends.

On the topic of death, Zib died peacefully. It was in a way a blessing because his sciatica had been really causing him a lot of pain. We've heard three scripture readings on death. Isaiah pictures it as something God is going to eliminate at the end of time (he will destroy death forever and wipe away the tears from all faces) and to those who have remained faithful, God will provide a wonderful banquet (and since death and tears – including such things as starvation - will be done away with, the banquet will be unending).

Paul tells us in the second reading about Christ's second coming. The Thessalonians were worried that their friends and family who had already died would miss out on the grand event of Jesus' return at the end of time. Paul said, don't worry, those who have already died will rise first then all of us together will be taken up to meet our Lord, our king, visibly enthroned in glory.

In the gospel Jesus assures us there's plenty of room in God's great kingdom and he will have a place ready for those who follow him. We will be with him always. The words of the gospel we just heard come from the Last Supper, shortly before Jesus' arrest. With the conviction that his followers would be with him always, he tells them "do not let your hearts be troubled." It was easy for Jesus to say, but hard to do for the apostles considering what they were soon going to have to face.

Jesus always says to us during difficult times: "do not let your hearts be troubled." The loss of Zib is sad. He had so many talents and so many good qualities. Now, instead of having the support of his inspiration and encouragement, we have to let go, we have to say goodbye. But it's only a temporary goodbye. As we follow the way, the truth and the life, we will all meet again in the everlasting kingdom of God's love. May our faith be strong and may our hearts not be troubled, and as Zib would say to us if he were to leave us with any words of wisdom: "try to be nice."

15th Sunday in Ordinary Time
July 12, 2015

INTRODUCTION – (*Amos 7, 12-15; Ephesians 1, 3-10; Mark 6, 7-13*) Our first reading today comes from the prophet Amos. Amos lived about 700 years before Christ. By that time, the Kingdom of God had been divided into two kingdoms. His prophetic message was to the northern kingdom that they would soon be destroyed unless the people reformed their lives. His message of reform was not well received. No one likes to be told that they are not living the way God wants them to live. In understanding today's passage, it helps to know that at that time there were professional prophets; that is, some people made their living by telling people how to solve their problems, giving them advice, predicting the future, etc. These professional prophets were often servants of pagan gods - not servants of the God of Abraham. They usually spoke the kinds of things their clients would want to hear because if they offended or rebuked their client, they would not have been paid their fee. Amos preached at the sanctuary in Bethel where there was a temple in competition with the Temple in Jerusalem. The high priest in Bethel, Amaziah, mistook Amos for one of the professional prophets and told him to go back to Jerusalem where he came from. Amos protested that he was not a career prophet. He patiently explained that he was living a nice peaceful life as a farmer and God called him to go to Bethel and warn the people that their sinful lives would lead to destruction. Today's passage prepares us for the gospel where Jesus sends his apostles out to preach and warns them that their message will not always be well received.

HOMILY – I'm sure most people know by now that Fr. Lammeier passed away this past Monday. We had been blest by Fr. Lammeier's willingness to help us here for the past 15 years. He wrote in his will his (quote) "request that the homilist talk on 'death' or the priesthood. Please no eulogy. There is not an awful lot of good that can be said, and I would want the homily to be a little longer than that." (unquote). Contrary to his quoted comments, there is an awful lot of good that could be said. He was a very humble man, highly respected, had a good sense of humor, worked hard on his homilies and described himself as a simple priest who said his prayers and did his work He influenced many people by his wisdom, whether they were the archbishops he served as administrative secretary, Archbishops Leibold and Bernardin, or whether he was ministering to the ordinary parishioner who came to him with a question or to confession on Saturday afternoon. I know that he enjoyed helping out here and he enjoyed the people he met here. Several times I invited him to live here and about two years ago, he accepted my offer, primarily because he could no longer stay by himself. Last fall he had to move to a nursing home because he could no longer walk. I saw him last Saturday and he looked fine, except he complained about his sciatica causing him a great deal of pain. Last Monday he got up, concelebrated Mass at the nursing home (which meant so much to him). As the day went on he kept declining until he passed away. Often when people visited him, instead of saying "goodbye" he always said "try to be nice." I am sure if he were here physically right now, his last words would not be "goodbye" but he would say to us: "try to be nice." It's a good imperative for all of us to follow.

In our gospel today, Jesus began to send his apostles out to heal the sick, to preach repentance and to expel demons. Notice how Mark words this: he "began to send them out" implying that he will continue to do so, and he does, even today. Fr. Lammeier was certainly one of those who generously and unselfishly gave himself to that ministry. Another person who has served the Church and who has served us with an abundance of generosity and competence is Carol Roosa. (She has retired as business manager as most of you know.) Carol has been a great blessing to me and to St. Boniface. For the past couple of years she has been coaching her daughter, Jenni, and preparing her to take over as business manager. Jenni is a very competent young lady and I am sure she will do a fantastic job.

Let us consider another idea that is important in today's gospel, an idea we should take home with us. Jesus tells those he sent out to travel light, just wearing the clothes on their back. In Mark's gospel they were permitted to also have a staff and sandals. They didn't need a lot of stuff because they needed to learn to depend on God for food and for a place to sleep. We don't have to go to that extreme, but truth is, most of us could get by with fewer things. I think the most important lesson buried in today's gospel is not how much stuff we have, but how much stuff fills our calendars. We keep ourselves so busy that we never have time to pray or too often prayer gets dumped at the end of the day. When we get to the end of the day, we're too tired. That's something I have to struggle with too. We may not be called to go out and preach and heal and expel demons, but we are all called to holiness, and we can't get holy unless we pray. Think about it as you are putting together your "to do" list. Does prayer have a place on it? Thank you for taking the time to be here today to honor our Lord and Creator in prayer. Amen.

16th Sunday in Ordinary Time
July 19, 2015

INTRODUCTION – (*Jeremiah, 23, 1-6; Ephesians, 2, 13-18; Mark 6, 30-34*) Our first reading comes from Jeremiah the prophet who lived during the years of the Babylonian conquest and exile of Israel, about 600 years before Christ. In this passage, Jeremiah is speaking to the Jewish kings and leaders of his day. He refers to them as shepherds, an image that goes back to around the time of Abraham hundreds of years before Jeremiah. Jeremiah denounces the Jewish kings and leaders as useless and evil shepherds who cared only about themselves. It was their failure to guide God's people in God's ways that led to the Babylonian exile and the destruction of many people, the nation, and the Temple. In today's passage, God promises he himself would make sure that good shepherds would take over and caring for his people. However, God's promise that "the days are coming" took a long time to come; not just the 50 years of exile in Babylon, but 600 years before the king would arrive who would govern wisely and who would save Judah. We hear about this king in today's gospel, a good shepherd who guides hundreds and thousands of people who flock to him looking for wisdom and guidance. Notice the emphasis on the concept that he guides them by his teaching. Unfortunately, our history tells us his own people eventually turned away from him, but he continues to be shepherd for millions of people from all over the world.

HOMILY – The apostles have been busy. Last week we heard that Jesus had sent them out to preach repentance, to cast out demons and to heal the sick. Jesus warned them that their mission could be difficult, they might be rejected or worse. It must have been a good experience for it sounds as if they came back to Jesus very excited about their experience. But they were tired too. Jesus recognizes that and, like the good shepherd that he is, he suggests they take some time to rest to regain their energy. It doesn't work. A big crowd of people figured out where he was headed and were waiting for him by the time Jesus and the apostles got there. We do not know who all these people were, people who dropped everything, not even thinking about their next meal, so they could see and hear Jesus. My suspicion is these were people from the neighboring villages which the apostles had just visited. I had always felt that Jesus didn't send the Apostles off on a far trip since it was their first try at evangelizing.

Jesus, who had intended to be a good shepherd for his Apostles in giving them a little time to rest, now becomes a good shepherd for these people, recognizing their need for good leadership. St. Mark tells us they were like sheep without a shepherd and Jesus was touched by their needs and he reached out to help them. I think it's really significant to notice how he chose to help them. The gospel tells us "he began to teach them many things." We're told in the other gospels he healed many who were sick and then, because it was late, he made sure they all (5000 of them) got a full meal. The mention of the meal gets us ahead of ourselves and I want to stick with the passage we just heard – especially the last verse which tells us Jesus' "heart was moved with pity for them, for they were like sheep without a shepherd; and he began to teach them many things."

I am sure religion classes in grade school, high school, perhaps college or perhaps the RCIA have been part of our educational training. It's really easy, when we get out of school, to think now I know enough. I remember when I taught religion in high school. If I went over some material that the students were taught in grade school, they really complained about it. With a rebellious tone they informed me "we don't need to learn about this, we learned this in grade school." Of all the saints I have ever read about, not one of them thought they knew enough about Christ. Every one of them continued to learn more and more about Christ and about their faith through prayer, through readings, through sermons, through conversations, through learning how to practice it better and through any way they could (even through suffering). When we reach the pearly gate, God's not going to bring us a second grade test to see if we can pass it; God's going to look at us to see how holy we've become. Everyone's vocation is holiness.

In the responsorial psalm today we prayed Psalm 23, the best known and probably best loved of all 150 psalms. It looks at life the way sheep would look at it and it tells us what great blessings God has for us.

The idea I want to leave with you is that the teaching of Jesus is the door to that paradise God promises us. Here are the steps that will get us there. Letting ourselves be taught by him allows us to get to know him. That's just like any good teacher who may have influenced us along the way. The more we know him, the more we want to get to know him. The more we get to know him, the more we discover that we love him. It is in that loving relationship with him that we will enjoy the blessings we hear about in Psalm 23. Letting Jesus teach us, through prayer, through readings, through sermons, through conversations, through practicing our faith better and through any way possible (even suffering) is the first step to the fullness of life that he came to offer us. Amen.

17th Sunday in Ordinary Time
July 26, 2015

HOMILY – *(2 Kings 4:42-22; Ephesians 4:1-6; John 6:1-15)* I suspect only a few people may have noticed that today's gospel came from John. We have been following Mark's gospel this year, and in Mark's gospel we have come to the account of Jesus feeding a multitude of 5000 men. (Women and children might at least double that number.) Mark's description of the feeding of the multitude is very brief, whereas, John's account leads into a lengthy and beautiful discourse on Jesus as the bread of life. Thus our readings have switched over to John for a few weeks.

Imagine yourself as part of that huge crowd when Jesus and the apostles start passing out food. You would surely ask yourself or someone nearby: What is happening? Where is all this food coming from? Would you be impressed? Impressed enough to remember that it happened? The early followers of Jesus were impressed enough to tell the story over and over – to such an extent that it is the only miracle found in all four gospels, and in Matthew and Mark there are two accounts of the miracle. Scholars think it is most probably a different version or rendition of the same event.

The gospels do not tell us how Jesus worked this miracle. But if you stop and think about it, there are only about one or two miracles where the gospels describe how Jesus did it, like maybe when he put mud on the eyes of the man born blind (*Jn.* 9) or put his finger into the ears of the deaf mute person. Most of the time, however, Jesus just healed a person with a word or with the touch of his hand. Somehow, Jesus fed all the people along with having lots of food left over. If a person doesn't accept this was miraculous, then they probably would not accept any of the miracles Jesus worked. They would decide according to their own whim what is and what isn't historical about the gospels.

Jesus' concern for the people was described in last week's gospel which told us "his heart was moved with pity for them, for they were like sheep without a shepherd." Just as God miraculously fed his people in the desert when he rescued them from slavery in Egypt, so now he feeds them again. It shows God cares about our most basic needs and will help us if we go to him. Sometimes we think we can handle everything all by ourselves and we don't need his help, but we do. We can't let ourselves forget the famous line Jesus spoke at the Last Supper: "without me you can do nothing." (*Jn. 5,15*) We know we do not always get what we ask for, but we have to trust that we will get what God thinks is best for us. No prayer is ever wasted. On the other hand, we also can't let ourselves forget, that although Jesus can and does step in when we need his help, he also expects us to reach out and help one another. Who knows, if a person is in need, God may have chosen to use us. We might be the exact answer to someone else's prayers when we reach out. When God chooses to use us, we can do great things, just as, with Jesus' help, the little food the boy in the gospel offered was enough to feed a multitude of people.

The hungry people in the world do depend on those who have been more generously blessed to share some of their blessings. Thus we have mission collections, the St. Vincent de Paul, Churches Active in Northside, Catholic Relief Services, food stamps and an almost infinite number of charitable and government organizations that help the poor. I'm not going to try to solve the problem of world hunger today. I just mention this so no one thinks: "well if Jesus can feed all those hungry people, why should I give out my hard earned money. I'll go to tonight's game instead. Let Jesus feed them."

Jesus did not come to hand out fish sandwiches. He did come to teach us to "love one another." If he wanted to hand out food all day, he would have allowed the people to make him their king. We might think Jesus would have found it flattering if everyone wanted him to be their king, to have people bowing to him, getting people to do whatever he wanted a little more easily. But in the gospel, their wanting him to be their king was a kind of rejection of Jesus. It was a rejection in that the people didn't want to accept him on his terms. They wanted to accept him on their terms. Their terms were that he would always be around to meet all their needs, especially their political needs: independence from the Romans and sending the Romans back to Italy. Jesus had a different agenda than being the people's king. He wants to meet our needs but in a different way than giving everyone whatever they want. He wants to feed us with the bread of life, eternal life. St. John in his gospel refers to this miracle of feeding the multitude as a "sign." Like any sign it points to something else. We will hear a lot about the meaning of this sign in the next few weeks.

18th Sunday in Ordinary Time
August 2, 2015

INTRODUCTION – (*Exodus 16:2-4,12-15; Ephesians 4: 17, 20-24; John 6: 24-35*) Last Sunday we heard about Jesus feeding a great multitude of thousands of people with five loaves of bread and two fish. The people were so impressed by this miracle that they wanted to make him their king. Even if Jesus thought that keeping people's stomachs full was perhaps a nice idea, he knew that's not what his ministry was all about. It's not why God the Father sent him into this world. His mission was to change hearts, a mission that threatened the power and position of the religious leaders of his day. The disciples, of course, would have been excited about Jesus being king (they would end up with an important position in the kingdom), so he sent them off in their boat, away from the enthusiastic crowd. He then slipped away from everyone and went to a mountain alone to pray. Later on, in the middle of the night, Jesus came walking on the surface of the water and joined his apostles. Eventually, their boat arrived at Capernaum. It was at Capernaum that the people caught up with him. That's where our gospel begins.

In their conversation with Jesus, the people bring up the topic of God feeding his people with Manna in the desert, 1300 years earlier, when they left Egypt and were headed to the promised land. Our first reading is about the Manna in the desert because it is mentioned in the gospel.

HOMILY – I mentioned in my introduction that after Jesus fed the multitude miraculously, the people wanted to make him a king. The apostles would have loved that idea, so Jesus sent them off in their boat and he went off to pray. He did return to them walking on the surface of the water, and stayed with them as they reached Capernaum. The people finally caught up with Jesus there. They tried to find out how and when he got there. I say all this so you can see the important connection between the feeding of the multitude and the conversation about it that followed. The people start the conversation by asking when Jesus arrived at Capernaum and immediately Jesus takes the conversation to a deeper level. Jesus knew why they were looking for him, they got a free meal, but they did not understand that what Jesus had done in the feeding was a sign – a sign that would have a message for them.

So let's reflect on signs for a moment. They are so important because they are the primary way by which we communicate with one another. Thus, our lives are surrounded by signs. Not just store signs or street signs, but also the subtle signs we give one another like a smile or a look of disappointment or anger. Even the very words I'm using are signs. For example, if I say the word "elephant," the image of an elephant comes into your mind. If I were speaking in Greek, or we were driving through China, the signs would not communicate with us. We wouldn't know what they were trying to tell us. Jesus had just fed a great multitude, but it was meant to tell the people something. They didn't catch its meaning and what Jesus was talking about. He tells them "do not labor for food that perishes." Of course, we do have to labor for our food. God told Adam after he ate the forbidden fruit that he would have to "earn your bread by the sweat of your brow." (*Gen. 3,19*) But Jesus wanted the people to know there are things even more important than having something to eat when we're hungry. "What things?" a person without any spiritual vision might ask. Jesus' answer is that it is food that he's willing to offer us, food that will satisfy us and bring us eternal life. This is what Jesus has to offer. God the Father himself has put his guarantee (his seal) on Jesus' ministry and on the great gift that Jesus has to offer.

Next it seems as if the people are asking "if you offer this food that endures for eternal life, how do we get some? What does God want us to do in order to have this special food." Jesus' answer, "believe in the one he sent." As they begin to catch on that Jesus is asking them to believe in him, they ask "what are you going to do to make us believe in you?" This is where they introduce the idea of the Manna. God gave their ancestors Manna (bread from heaven) while they were in the desert, maybe they wanted Jesus to do something greater. Jesus said "no, I am the real bread from heaven...which gives life to the world." (Notice here is one of the "I am" statements which we find so frequently in John's gospel.)

Before we close the book on today's gospel, I want to reflect on two other important words in this section: the words "work" and "believe." The people ask "what can we do to accomplish the works of God." Jesus said "believe in the one he sent." Basically, if we are going to have faith (and live our faith – they're both the same thing), it takes work. So many people I have counselled want living their faith to be easy, to never have their faith challenged by hard times or by difficult people. I truly think that many people have an unexpected expectation that if I do everything God wants, then God should do everything I want. There is a ring of fairness to that. Well, God doesn't always do everything we want and God didn't promise to make the road easy; he just promised he would always be with us. For example, God doesn't always make us feel excited about getting up on Sunday to go to Mass; we might prefer to stay in bed or watch TV. Or if it's time to pray, do we jump for joy or do we feel like we do when it's time to exercise. God doesn't always make it easy to forgive someone who hurt us or to love that disagreeable relative or neighbor. God doesn't always make it easy to be pure or generous or humble or to face the truth about ourselves when we know we're wrong but we don't want to admit it. Are these things work? Not always, but sometimes they are. I think that's given us enough to think about regarding today's gospel (three words: signs, faith and work). So, we'll leave it there with this promise that we will reflect on Jesus as the bread of eternal life in much greater depth in the next few weeks.

19th Sunday in Ordinary Time
August 9, 2015

INTRODUCTION – (*I Kings 19,4-8; Ephesians 4,30; John 6, 41-51*) Jezebel was an evil queen who reigned in Israel eight hundred fifty years before Christ. One of her many goals in life was to eliminate faith and worship of Yahweh, the God of Israel. At the same time in Israel, there also lived the prophet Elijah who was dedicated to serving Yahweh. Naturally, these two would collide. Just previous to today's first reading from the Book of Kings, Elijah had worked a powerful miracle on Mt. Carmel, a place now known as Haifa, which dramatically demon-strated in the presence of the King, 450 of the pagan priests, and all the people of Israel, that Yahweh was truly God and that the gods Jezebel promoted were non-existent. Jezebel, instead of being converted, became a sore loser. She sent her army after Elijah to kill him. Elijah quickly got out of town. He ran to the desert in southern Judea and this is where we meet him in today's first reading. He is hungry, tired, deeply depressed and hoping to die. However, God did not desert his faithful prophet. Instead, God sent Elijah to the same mountain in Sinai where God had given Moses the 10 Commandments, that is, to Mt. Sinai, aka Mt. Horeb.

This passage has been chosen because it speaks of a special food God gave Elijah, a food that sustained him in his journey to Mt. Horeb for 40 days and 40 nights. The passage connects with the gospel where Jesus tells us he is the bread that will strengthen us on our journey through life and into eternal life.

HOMILY – My intent today is to try to pull together what we've already heard from the sixth chapter of St. John's gospel and to tie it together with what is yet to come. The sixth chapter of John begins with the account of Jesus feeding over 5000 people in a miraculous way. After this demonstration, the people decided they wanted to make him their king. Not only had he fed people, but he healed people. They were smart enough to know they would have a good thing going if they had Jesus as their king. But Jesus had a mission that was bigger than what the people had in mind – he came to save the world, not just one group of people or even one nation – and his mission of salvation would lead to salvation that would last forever. So Jesus stealthily slipped away from the crowd.

When the people found Jesus a short time later, he explained to them that there's lots more to life than getting free health care and having free food to eat every day. "Do not work for food that perishes but for the food that endures for eternal life, which the Son of Man will give you," we heard him say in last week's gospel. Jesus sounds as if he's not being practical – but he is very practical. We do have to be concerned about our everyday material needs, and we need to be concerned about the needs of others who cannot provide for themselves. Recall it is the same Jesus who told us that we will be judged on such criteria as "I was hungry and you gave me to eat, thirsty and you gave me to drink, naked and you clothed me, etc." In this passage from John's gospel, Jesus wants us to see the bigger picture. There is a whole other life and a whole other world beyond this present life, a life that will have no ending, and as we journey through this life, we must prepare for what comes next.

Jesus came to reveal that world to us. The bread and fish he had recently fed the crowd was a sign, a sign of something of much greater value he had to give. What he offers is greater than any miracle of feeding we read about in the Old Testament; such as, we heard in today's first reading or God feeding the Hebrew people with manna. The people pretty much followed what Jesus was saying up to this point. They wanted Jesus to feed them with bread from heaven until Jesus informed them he was that bread. "I am bread that came down from heaven," he tells them. In order to enjoy the benefits of what he had to offer, he says we have to believe in him. They found that hard to accept. It contradicted what they knew – they were sure that Jesus didn't come down from heaven. They knew his human origins, his mother and his father. In their certainty, they were blind to knowing who Jesus truly was. Today's gospel was a little difficult to follow, but this is the key to understanding it: that Jesus really did come down from the Father in heaven.

Jesus kept insisting on this. He told them listening and learning from God would make it possible for them to have faith in Jesus. The implication is that the crowd failed to listen and learn from God and preferred to murmur about what Jesus was saying. This is saying to us that Jesus is the bread of life for us when we learn from him, when we pray to him, when we follow his ways. He nourishes our spirit with his spirit, his wisdom and his love. In those ways he feeds us. As hard as it was for the people to accept Jesus as the bread of life that has come down from heaven, whom they are to believe in, Jesus really blew their mind when he said further "the bread I will give is my flesh." This is another way he feeds us, not just through having faith in him, but feeding us with his body and blood, a special unity with him that we will reflect on next week. Amen.

Vigil & Feast of the Assumption
August 14/15, 2000

INTRODUCTION AT THE VIGIL – (*1 Chronicles 15:3-4, 15-16; 16:1-2; 1 Corinthians 15:5b- 57; Luke 11:27-28*) It is a dogma of our faith that at the end of her life, Mary, like her son, was taken body and soul into heaven. This is the meaning of the Assumption, whose vigil we celebrate this evening.

Our first reading is about the Ark of the Covenant, the sacred gold plated box that contained the Ten Commandments and on top of which were two golden angels (similar to the two angels on our tabernacle doors if you can see them.) The Ark was the unique symbol of God's presence with Israel. It was constructed in the desert after Moses and the Israelites left Egypt. It led them into the Promised Land. Often it was taken into battle with them. When King David established his capital in Jerusalem about the year 1000 BC, he brought the Ark there. Today's reading describes this solemn and joyful occasion. After the temple was built, the Ark was placed in the Holy of Holies and there it remained for 400 years until the Babylonians destroyed the temple. In Christian symbolism, Mary is sometimes referred to as the Ark of the Covenant. As the Ark represented the special presence of God dwelling with his people, Mary carried within herself Jesus who is truly Son of God dwelling with us.

INTRODUCTION ON THE FEAST – (*Rev 11:19a; 12:1-6a, 10ab; 1 Corinthians 15:20-27; Luke 1: 39-56*) It is a dogma of our faith that at the end of her life, Mary, like her son, was taken body and soul into heaven. This is the meaning of the Assumption, the feast we celebrate today.

In our first reading from Revelation, we hear about a woman, a child and a dragon. The dragon is the devil and the powers of evil at work in the world. The child is Christ. The woman in our reading has a double symbolism. She stands for Mary, the physical mother of Jesus Christ and she stands for the Church, our spiritual mother who brings Jesus Christ to birth in us through faith and the sacraments. The glorious way in which the woman is described has a double symbolism too. It symbolizes the glory of Mary in the assumption and it also symbolizes the glory which we, the faithful, the Church, hope to enjoy one day.

HOMILY – St. Francis de Sales asks the simple question in his sermon for the Assumption: "What son would not bring his mother back to life and would not bring her into paradise after her death if he could?" Who could argue with a statement like that? In Mary's Assumption the glory of Jesus' resurrection is first of all extended to his mother, but as we celebrate it we celebrate likewise our own hope to share in this risen glory some day. We recite this belief in the last lines of the creed: "We believe in the resurrection of the dead, and the life of the world to come."

It's interesting that the Holy Father declared the dogma of the Assumption during a difficult time in recent history. In 1950, when the doctrine of the

Assumption was declared by Pope Pius XII, we had experienced two world wars, the Holocaust, the Atomic Bomb and the beginning of the Cold War. The world had enough reason to feel hopeless. Contrasted with the pessimism of the time, this dogma offers hope, hope that the destiny of the human race is more than wars, destruction and devastation. At about that same time in 1950, the cult of the body and the glories of sexuality were beginning to take hold of society. The Church leaders could see that the more that sex and the body were idolized the more society would lose its respect for marriage and family values. In contrast to the glorification of the body as an object of pleasure, this dogma affirms the true dignity and the beauty of the body and the source of that dignity and beauty which is God's grace within us.

In the Assumption Mary is fully united with her son in glory. She remains his mother. He remains her son. Cardinal Suenens once said, "Jesus does not point out Mary and say, 'She used to be my mother.'" Not only is she Jesus' mother, she is our mother too, for on Calvary Jesus gave her to us to be our mother. "Woman, behold your son," he said to her and to St. John, who was a representative of all disciples, Jesus said "Behold your mother." We know and believe that Mary is concerned about our salvation. We expect Mary to help us and we pray to her. Protestants sometimes have trouble with this idea of praying to Mary. Jesus is our savior and we all believe that. But Protestants believe we should pray for one another. If we can ask others to pray for us and we pray for them, why can't those in heaven also pray for us? Are we now so separated from those who have died so that they no longer can help us or be concerned about us? If we seek the prayers of sinners on earth, for we are all sinners, why not seek the intercession of the saints in heaven? Why not turn to the Queen of saints, God's own Mother?

The Assumption tells us that God is not only concerned about our souls but also about our bodies. They are temples of the Spirit. They are part of who we are, and so the feast of the Assumption is a feast that celebrates who we shall be.

In addition to the Arc of the Covenant being a symbol for Mary, there is an another way in which today's first reading connects with today's feast. In Christian literature, especially in the book of Revelation, Jerusalem symbolizes our heavenly home. Thus, the Ark being taken to Jerusalem symbolized Mary being taken body and soul into the heavenly kingdom.

20th Sunday in Ordinary Time
August 16, 2015

INTRODUCTION – (*Proverbs 9, 1-6; Ephesians 5, 15-20; John 6, 51-58*) In the Book of Proverbs, wisdom is symbolized as a person and is referred to as Lady Wisdom. She is pictured as the owner of an inn. The columns that are part of her house symbolize stability, while the number seven symbolizes perfection. In today's reading, she is busy inviting people to lodge at her guesthouse and partake of the food she has prepared. Those who accept her invitation will be rewarded with joy and an abundance of life. In the gospel, Jesus invites us to partake of the food he offers, his flesh and blood, so that we may enjoy the fullness of life.

HOMILY – Today's gospel is one of the most controversial and hotly debated passages in John's gospel. (*The New Interpreter's Bible – Vol IX –pg 605*) John began chapter six by telling us about Jesus feeding a great crowd of people (over 5000) with five loaves of bread and a couple of dried fish. Jesus and John called this miracle a "sign." For the last two weeks, we have heard Jesus interpret the meaning of this sign. Having faith in Jesus has been the main focus of what had been said about the meaning of this sign so far. For example, two weeks ago we heard Jesus say: "I am the bread of life; whoever comes to me will never hunger, and whoever **believes** in me will never thirst." Or "this is the work of God, that you **believe** in the one he sent."

You might have noticed by now, there is no mention of the fish. Bread has become the main subject of the gospel passages we've been hearing. It's not bread that will satisfy our hunger for a few hours, however, that Jesus offers us. It is bread from heaven that Jesus wants to give us, bread that gives life to the world. That bread is Jesus – "I am the bread of life," he tells us. Without forgetting what Jesus said about **believing** in him, faith in Jesus is really important. As you will see, believing in him becomes even more challenging regarding what I'm going to say next. Today's passage introduces another important element in interpreting the meaning of the sign of the multiplication of the loaves. Jesus tells us in today's gospel, "the bread that I will give is my **flesh** for the life of the world," and he insists we are to eat his flesh and drink his blood.

This idea really caused a stir among his hearers, but Jesus repeated it again and again. Six times in the next six verses he tells us we must feed on this bread if we want to enter into eternal life. This is where there is all the controversy. Because not all Christians believe what we believe as Catholics, they have to find a way to explain away what Jesus says. Many Christian denominations say Jesus is only speaking symbolically, and he does not mean for us to take him literally. Those who think Jesus was speaking symbolically would also have to consider he was speaking symbolically at the Last Supper when he said "take, eat; this is my body;...drink...this is my blood." (Mt 26,26-28). That would have made for a strange meal with Jesus saying eat and drink, but only eat and drink symbolically. It would be like someone inviting you for dinner and serving you bread and water and telling you this is a symbol of steak and fine wine. If Jesus were speaking symbolically, he would not have allowed many of his followers to walk away because they thought he was out of his mind. He would have called them to come back and say, "wait, you are taking me literally." He knew they were leaving because they were taking him literally, and that's the way he wanted to be understood.

When Jesus said: "this bread is my flesh which I will give for the life of the world," his hearers asked: "How can this man give us his flesh to eat?" "How can this be?" is what we all have asked ourselves at times. In answering that question for myself I just remind myself that God's word has power to create things and to change things. In the beginning of the Bible, God said, "let there be light, let there be plants, fish, birds, animals, etc." and there were. Jesus' words had the power to change things. He could change the weather (calming a storm on the sea), he could change sick and infirm people into well people, he could change a few loaves of bread and a couple of fish into enough to feed a huge crowd of hungry people. When he said this is my body, this is the cup of my blood, do this in memory of me, I believe in the power of those words. Another thing that helps my faith is to think of this: there is energy in bread and wine (and all other foods) and that's what gives us energy. At Mass the energy that is in the bread and wine is replaced by a divine form of energy that feeds the life of God that has been given to us in baptism. When we receive Communion, we don't usually feel much of a change any more than we might not feel a great surge of health and energy when we eat a healthy meal, but through Jesus the bread of life, we are being prepared for eternal life. In all of this, we cannot forget what our Lord said to Thomas after the resurrection: "blessed are those who have not seen and yet believe." That's us.

So, stay tuned. We have one more section of Chapter six which gives us a fuller account of the people's reaction to what Jesus said. Amen.

21st Sunday in Ordinary Time
August 23, 2015

INTRODUCTION – (*Joshua 24,1-2a,15-17,18b; Ephesians 5,21-32; John 6,60-69*) Shortly after Moses led God's people to the Promised Land, Moses died and Joshua took over the position Moses had held. In our reading today, Joshua gathered God's people together to renew their covenant with Yahweh. They enthusiastically chose to commit themselves to follow God faithfully. History has shown that later generations did not remain so faithful or so enthusiastic. The enthusiasm of God's people in today's first reading is contrasted with the unenthusiastic response of many who **had** been following Jesus until he taught them that he was the bread of life. They started walking away thinking he was talking nonsense. To their credit, the apostles, who did not understand Jesus any better than the crowd, stayed with Jesus for they had accepted that Jesus was the Holy One of God.

Today's Letter to the Ephesians, the second reading, encourages married couples to live a life of mutual love and such love will bring them supreme joy.

HOMILY – In last Sunday's gospel, we heard Jesus tell us (over and over) that we must eat his flesh and drink his blood. If we do not, we will not have life within us, we will not be raised up in the resurrection on the last day, we will not remain united with Christ, we will not share in God's life. That was a quick summary of last Sunday's gospel which we need to keep in mind in order to better understand today's gospel. Many in Jesus' audience thought Jesus was crazy. How could they eat his flesh and drink his blood, they asked. They were not cannibals and Jews especially were prohibited from consuming any kind of blood. They carefully drained all the blood from an animal before they prepared it for a meal. This is a very strict part of their kosher diet. They believed that life was in the blood and since life came from God, it needed to return to God and could not be consumed. Jesus turned this idea completely around when he said drink my blood, indicating that through the Eucharist we will share in his life, just as he shares in the life of the living Father.

What Jesus was saying on that occasion is the same thing he said at the Last Supper: "take, eat; this is my body;...drink...this is my blood." Some scholars question whether Jesus gave this teaching in the gospel or on some other occasion, perhaps even at the Last Supper. They speculate that over the course of time, today's gospel teaching was moved to its present location in John's gospel. Do not be surprised that these words of Jesus on the Eucharist may have been spoken at some other time because the gospels were formed in the early Church by remembering and reflecting on the words and deeds of Jesus, and they didn't always try to get everything in historical sequence. Rather, one event may have called to mind something similar, just as happens when we gather with friends and relatives at Thanksgiving or Christmas and we get to reminiscing about a loved one who died, and we tell about the things we remember. Eventually these remembrances were written down often in thematic sequence rather than in historical sequence some 35 to 60 years after Jesus had ascended into heaven.

The important message for us today is not exactly when Jesus gave us his teaching on the Eucharist but the reaction it produced. We see that many who were initially impressed with Jesus started walking away. Jesus knew they were taking him literally, that we must eat his flesh and drink his blood, and they thought he was saying crazy things. He didn't try to call them back. He knew what people thought and he wanted them to understand him literally. The Apostles didn't understand him either, but they believed in him and somehow knew his words were true. I think people who have a problem believing in the Eucharist are not really having a problem with the Eucharist as such. Even though they can't see or experience anything special, they are really having a problem with believing that Jesus is the Holy One of God. If you can accept that Jesus is God, then it's easier to accept what he says or does, even if you don't fully understand it. Ultimately a problem with faith in the Eucharist is a problem with faith in the incarnation, that Jesus is God who has taken on our human flesh so he could speak to us and show us, in a way we could understand, the way to eternal life. Amen.

22nd Sunday in Ordinary Time
August 30, 2015

INTRODUCTION – (*Deuteronomy 4:1-2,6-8; James 1: 17-18,21-22,27; Mark 7:1-8,14-15,21-23*) Today's first reading takes us back to the time of Moses, about 1300 years before Christ. Moses knew he would die before God's people could enter the Promised Land. So he gives the people some last minute instructions before they cross the Jordan. In essence, he is telling God's people that God loves them and he wants them to prosper. They will do so only if they keep God's laws. This passage fits well with our other two readings which teach us how important it is to obey God, both for our well-being in this world and our eternal happiness in the next.

HOMILY – As soon as we start to read today's gospel, we sense there is going to be a battle between Jesus and the Jewish leaders. Some Pharisees and scribes from Jerusalem came to see him. The presence of the scribes is what gives it away that there is going to be a confrontation. The scribes in those days would be like the lawyers of today – they were experts in the law. They had come a long way to find Jesus. They were from Jerusalem we are told, and Jerusalem was about a four days journey on foot. They observed that some of his disciples were eating without having washed their hands. It's interesting they didn't accuse Jesus of doing the same thing. Maybe he was finished eating, maybe he was busy teaching, maybe he remembered to wash his hands. Now, if they had a mother like mine, they would surely have remembered to wash their hands; it is a very good habit to have. But for the Jews, it was more than just a good habit to prevent germs. For the Jews, it was a religious tradition. It was like God turned away from you and was unhappy with you because you didn't wash your hands before eating. Mark tells us about lots of similar rules and regulations.

It's nice to learn that we have a God who is like a Jewish mother, concerned about everything we do. It's interesting to compare the God of Israel to the pagan gods that most other nations worshipped. Those gods were not real, of course, but in the thinking of those who worshipped them, their gods never paid much attention to what their devotees did. A person could do almost anything they wanted, and the gods didn't care as long as their worshippers gave them honor and offered appropriate sacrifice. Maybe that's partly why the Jews were often led into the worship of false gods. Pagan religion wasn't too demanding on them (unless you felt that your god was demanding that you sacrifice one of your children). But Yahweh, the God of Israel, had many rules about how his people were to live. There was more than the ten commandments; there were another 603 commandments dealing with all aspects of life. You can find them scattered about in the first five books of the Bible. Interestingly, the tradition about washing one's hands before eating was not one of the commandments (except for the priest). Handwashing before a meal was a tradition. Such traditions were believed to have come from Moses and Jewish teachers but were never written down. Jesus was being accused of not observing the tradition of the elders.

It was on this basis (that handwashing was a tradition) that Jesus responded to the Pharisees and scribes. They had come to embarrass him and to demonstrate that he was not teaching true doctrine. Jesus told his critics that they were the ones who were not teaching true doctrine because they allowed their traditions to overrule God's laws. Then Jesus turned to his crowd of listeners and made one of the most "revolutionary" statements he had ever made, and he made some big ones in his day. (cf Vawter, The Four Gospels, pg 188) He said: "nothing outside a person can enter and make a person unclean; rather the things that come out make that person unclean." (*vs. 15*) An editor gave us the interpretation of this: (*vs 19*) In this manner he declared all foods to be clean. This statement started a battle that the early Church fought over for many years before it was resolved.

Here we see Jesus, not just as a Jewish teacher, but as an authoritative teacher speaking with the divine authority to be able not only to interpret God's law but to change it. The Jewish diet was quite complicated and was seen as coming directly from God through Moses. Jesus, in one sentence, changed it all and clarified what it is that moves God to be unhappy with us. It is what comes out of our heart that makes God displeased with us, such as murder, theft, adultery, avarice, wickedness, licentiousness, envy and pride. In case you are wondering, licentiousness means lacking in moral restraint.

We do have a God who is concerned with the way we live, the way we treat others, and the respect and love we have for him. Too often we let our culture determine what is morally right or wrong rather than getting our sense of what is right and wrong from what God has spoken to us. Our religion is not always easy or convenient, but as Moses said to God's people centuries ago, "be careful to do as the Lord your God has commanded you...that you may live and prosper, and may have long life in the land which you are to possess." (*Exodus 5,32-33*) Amen.

23rd Sunday in Ordinary Time
September 6, 2015

INTRODUCTION – (*Isaiah 35:4-7; James 2:1-5; Mark 7:31-37*) In our first reading, we hear the prophet

Isaiah speaking words of encouragement to God's people during their captivity in Babylon. He proclaims: "Be strong, fear not! Here is your God...he comes to save you." God's salvation is expressed in terms of numerous blessings among which are healing the blind and the deaf, the lame and the mute. The reading prepares us for the gospel where Jesus heals a man who was a deaf mute. Jesus' healing work was a work of compassion, but it also announced in a dramatic way the saving presence of God among his people. In our own times of trial, we need to remind ourselves over and over that God is with us. In some way, even if we do not understand it, he is touching us with his saving love.

HOMILY – The basic belief of our faith is that Jesus saves; the very name "Jesus" means "God saves." If we do not know Jesus as a savior, we do not know Jesus at all. But what does he save us *from*? He saves us from many things. I can't say how many times I've felt Jesus' saving presence in avoiding a terrible accident while on the road. He saves us from sin and the effects of sin, perhaps from a strong temptation, a serious sickness, harm from someone who dislikes us. At the end of our lives, he brings those who love him into his kingdom of eternal life and assures us we will share in his risen life on the last day. These are just some of the ways he is our savior. Hopefully, you can see he is with us as our savior all through our lives and beyond into the next life. As he tells us in John's gospel, "I came that they may have life and may have it to the full." (*Jn 10,10*)

Yet this fullness of life unfolds gradually throughout our lives. When we reach the end of this present life, we will know in all its glory the fullness of life Christ came to bring us.

In today's gospel, we are shown how Jesus may touch us with his healing love if we ask him. I want to note especially two interesting features in today's gospel. First: we are told that the deaf man's family and friends "begged" Jesus to cure the man. What does that tell us about prayer? First of all, numerous people were involved here, asking for a favor from our Lord, and they didn't give up asking. They approached Jesus with a sense of urgency and expectation that Jesus would respond to their request. So, if we need Our Lord's help, we should enlist others to pray with us and most of all, we should not give up praying when we don't get what we want right away. Jesus even preached a couple of parables about praying without ceasing - that we are to keep on knocking when we need his help. People give up on God too fast. They are used to going into a store, buying what they want and leaving. When they don't get from God what they want instantaneously, they turn away and say "God just doesn't hear me."

The second thing interesting about this healing is that Jesus told the people not to tell anyone about it. There are various interpretations of what is called the Messianic secret, which is especially evident in Mark's gospel. One simple interpretation is that Jesus was not looking for fame or notoriety. He wasn't advertising in order to start a healing business. He wasn't trying to prove anything. He cared about people and wanted to help those who came to him for help. It's just what he did.

Not only did he heal people himself, he sent his disciples out to do the same thing. "They drove out many demons, and they anointed with oil many who were sick and cured them." (*Mark 6,13*) They were not always as successful as Jesus, but they did many good things.

We see in the *Acts of the Apostles* how Peter and Paul performed many miraculous deeds. Jesus promised his apostles: "Amen, Amen, I say to you, whoever believes in me will do the works that I do, and will do greater ones than these, because I am going to the Father." (*Jn. 14,12*)

The great St. Augustine who lived in the 5th century said that in his time, healings no longer happened because they were no longer necessary to spread the faith. However, toward the end of his life, he took back what he had said and described miraculous cures he had seen and which caused him to change his mind. (*Francis MacNutt, Healing, pg. 58*) Healings still happen if we don't give up on God too soon. I've seen them happen and I have great confidence in the Sacrament of the Sick and am happy to administer it when asked to do so. I believe in calling on medical professionals when necessary, but I also believe that today's gospel is telling us Jesus is still at work in the world, saving and healing. Amen.

24th Sunday in Ordinary Time
September 13, 2015

INTRODUCTION – (*Isaiah 50, 5-9; James 2, 14-18; Mark 8, 27-35*) The book of the prophet Isaiah contains four poems commonly referred to as Servant Songs. They are mysterious passages because no one is sure whom they referred to originally. They describe one whom God had chosen before birth - not only to serve God and to serve God's people in Israel, but to be a light for all of humanity. It's amazing how perfectly these Servant Songs, written over 500 years before Christ, describe Jesus. Today's passage describes how God's Servant would encounter resistance, persecution and martyrdom, and how God would stand by him during all his trials. We hear this same passage again on Palm Sunday and on Wednesday of Holy Week. It was chosen for today because we hear in today's gospel Jesus' first prediction that suffering, death and resurrection are ahead for him.

HOMILY – A married lady went out shopping one day and when she returned home she brought with her a beautiful dress. She showed it to her husband who almost had a stroke when he heard how much it cost. She agreed with him that it was very expensive, but she said she tried it on and she looked so beautiful in it she couldn't resist the temptation to buy it. Her husband told her you should have said: "get behind me, Satan." She said that's exactly what I said, and Satan said "you look fabulous from back here too!"

When Jesus told Peter: "get behind me, Satan," he wasn't calling Peter a devil. He was saying that Peter was doing Satan's job by trying to tempt Jesus away from following what Jesus knew was the Father's will for him - to suffer and to die for the redemption of the world. The Jewish people knew an anointed leader was coming who would save God's people. That anointed leader was called in Hebrew, Messiah and in Greek, the Christ. They expected, however, a powerful and glorious savior - not a suffering Messiah.

Peter answered rightly that Jesus was the Messiah, the Christ, but he didn't know about the suffering the Messiah would undergo. That's why Jesus didn't want the Apostles to tell anyone about him. They still had a lot to learn. Peter especially had to learn that Jesus was the Master and Teacher. Peter forgot he was Jesus' follower when he called Jesus aside and started to instruct Jesus that he would not have to go through any suffering. Jesus literally put Peter back in his place when he said, "get behind me." In other words, "you're not in charge, Peter. I called you to follow me, not tell me what to do."

Then he announced to everyone, if they wanted to follow Jesus, they would have to be willing to lose their life for him. In doing so, they would gain the fullness of life that Jesus came to bring. Today's gospel asks some very profound questions. It starts off asking "who is Jesus?" It ends up asking "who are you?" "Are you willing to give everything for Christ?" You will have nothing to lose and everything to gain. Amen.

25th Sunday in Ordinary Time
September 20, 2015

INTRODUCTION – (*Wisdom 2,12.17-20; James 3,16-4,3; Mark 9,30-37*) In 333 BC, Alexander the Great conquered everything between Egypt and India. For a little over 250 years, the Greeks controlled all of the Middle East including the Holy Land. The Greek rulers decided all nations under their rule should accept Greek culture and religion. The Jews were being forced to give up their belief in Yahweh, the one God they had served (not always faithfully) for 1500 years. Those who did not submit were persecuted or killed. Some of the Jews converted to Greek ways and pagan worship and some stayed faithful to Yahweh. Our first reading is from the Book of Wisdom, and in the reading it is the Jews who turned to paganism who are speaking. They plot against the faithful Jew, sarcastically refer to him or her as "the just one," and ridicule traditional faith in God. The first reading connects with the gospel in that Jesus, who is truly the "just one," predicts the suffering he will have to face for remaining faithful to God's work.

HOMILY – I don't know how many people play chess these days, but in the days before TV (if it's possible to imagine what the world was like way back then), and in the days before cell phones, ipads, etc., a person had to find a way of entertaining themselves. Our family enjoyed playing board games, cards and checkers. I especially enjoyed playing chess. For those unfamiliar with the game of chess, each player has 16 pieces and among those 16 pieces there are six different pieces, such as a king, a queen, castles, bishops, etc. The most important piece is the king. When your opponent attacks your king and he cannot be rescued, you've lost the game. The least important piece is a pawn. If your opponent captures one of your pawns, it could hurt you, but it's usually not fatal. I needed to explain this for the sake of a simple, but profound, lesson. The lesson is expressed in this old Italian proverb: "After the game, the king and the pawn go into the same box." In other words, no matter how important we are, or how rich or smart or successful, or how unimportant we are, we're all the same in one respect - death will take all of us. One person may be able to afford having a more expensive stone placed over his or her grave, but fortune gives us nothing which we can really own. The only thing we have that will truly be ours is the degree of love we've had for God and for others.

I think today's gospel is a perfect illustration of this truth. Jesus predicts, for the second time, the high price he will have to pay in order to be faithful to the mission that the Father sent him to do. Each of the apostles, on the other hand, are busy trying to prove which of them is the greatest. This was not just a childish game they were playing. Their discussion had real practical implications. They did not understand what the Kingdom of God really is. They imagined it to be an earthly kingdom where they would each have a place of importance. They were in the process of figuring out who would have the highest position in that kingdom, and the next highest, and so on.

Jesus' response to them was very gentle; he used a simple expression of affection for a child. In that culture, children were loved but they had no social standing and no rights. That's not much different to today's world where an infant has no rights, not even the right to live, until it is born. Using the child as an example of humility, Jesus says "if anyone wants to be first, he shall be the last of all and the servant of all." Then Jesus went further. He said this child, the lowest member of the human race on the social ladder, actually represented Jesus. Jesus said: "whoever welcomes one of these little children in my name welcomes me." Karl Barth describes what Jesus meant in this way: we are: "to think of every human being, even the oddest, most villainous or miserable as one to whom Jesus Christ is Brother and God is Father; and we have to deal with him (or her) on this assumption." Jesus' words should give joy and a sense of satisfaction to those who care for children: to parents, teachers, nurses and doctors, people who support the work of our schools, safety personnel like fire fighters and police, and pickets at abortion clinics.

You might wonder, does Jesus imply that we are to think of ourselves as having no worth or importance? Not at all. Jesus is interested in our being great, but he wants us to be great in the right way. We don't have to stand on a stage as if we're running for some office, touting our importance and brilliance and our qualifications. Nor do we have to hide our gifts and talents. Simply put, we should use them to serve others. Being great in Jesus' mind means to serve others. Jesus told his disciples at the Last Supper: "let the greatest among you be as the youngest, and the leader as the servant." To emphasize what he said, he adds: "I am among you as one who serves." (*Lk. 22,26-27*)

26th Sunday in Ordinary Time
September 27, 2015

HOMILY – (*Numbers 11:25-29; James 5:1-6; Mark 9:38-43,45,47-48*) A few years ago, a movie came out entitled Ben Hur. Some of you might remember it. Ben Hur, whose full name was Judah Ben Hur, was played by Charlton Heston. Judah Ben Hur and his family lived well in the city of Jerusalem. Even though Israel was under the control of the Romans, the Jewish family of Ben Hur had pride, prestige and privileges. A series of misfortunes led to the loss of their privileged position and Ben Hur's mother and sister were sent to the dungeons where they eventually contracted leprosy. Judah himself was condemned to slavery and was to work in the Roman galleys. In a chain gang with other slaves, he was being marched through the countryside to his doom. On the way they paused to rest in a small village. A local man, quiet and strong, gave a cup of cold water to the exhausted prisoner, Ben Hur. Ben Hur looked up to see who was being so kind to him, and he found himself gazing into the eyes of Jesus of Nazareth. He remembered Jesus' look forever and the kind favor Jesus had done for him.

A number of years later Ben Hur won back his honor and his position. He returned to Jerusalem and to his old family house. One day, a noisy procession passed in the street as a man was jostled and pushed along to his public execution, carrying a cross. Ben Hur was filled with compassion for this prisoner, so exhausted and hardly able to walk. When the condemned criminal fell, Ben Hur moved forward to help and lift the fallen man. Their eyes met, and once again Judah Ben Hur looked into the eyes of Jesus of Nazareth. Jesus' kind action offering Ben Hur a cup of water was rewarded by the compassion Ben

Hur learned to have for others who were suffering.

As Jesus passed on his way to Calvary, his shadow fell across two leper women in the crowd, the mother and sister of Judah Ben Hur. They were healed of their disease.

The story is not in the gospel but it makes a beautiful illustration of Jesus' words in today's gospel: "If anyone gives you a cup of water to drink, he will most certainly not lose his reward." The kindness of Ben Hur in running to help a fallen man was rewarded immediately through Jesus' shadow healing his mother and sister.

Jesus is telling us every good deed, even the least, will bring good things to us. God is faithful and God is not going to let us get ahead of him in being generous. Jesus reminds us also in today's gospel that every evil deed will bring us harm and that's why he warns us to get rid of evil in our lives now. He does not want us to literally cut off parts of our bodies (we would all be going around with parts missing if he did), but he is telling us even if something is near and dear to us, if it causes us to sin, we must not delay in changing things around. Fortunately when we repent of our sins, God forgets the wrong we have done. But he won't forget our good deeds. At the time of Jesus, the villages were rather small and people could better look out for one another. In our modern world we live in a village as large as the whole world and there are so many people in need that sometimes it's overwhelming. But we can't just close our eyes and hearts and we have to help as best we can with a cup of water or a kind word.

As people struggle under their crosses, we can reach out to help them. Looking into their eyes, we may see the eyes of Jesus of Nazareth. There will be times when we are in need of a cup of water or a kind word or a helping hand. Hopefully, someone will be there for us.

We have hundreds of opportunities to do good throughout the day. I would be remiss, however, if I did not mention a few areas here in our parish where you can do some good if you wish to. We do not hand out bottles of water as I have heard some churches do, but we provide a first class education to children, many of whom could not afford it. One of the things that enables us to do this ministry is our bingo and we're always needing helpers at our bingo. We also need coaches for sports teams, helpers at our festival, people to sing in the choir, people to visit the sick and shut-ins and to do other apostolic work through the Legion of Mary and people to help the poor through CAIN and our St. Vincent de Paul Society. Another very good thing we do here is we pray. More things are accomplished through prayer than any of us can imagine. If you want to do some good for others, here are some ideas.

Whatever good thing we do will be a blessing for someone, but it will be a blessing for ourselves as well. Every little thing we do is important. Even if our love is not received in a grateful manner, we will not lose our reward.

27th Sunday in Ordinary Time
October 4, 2015

HOMILY – (*Genesis 2,18-24; Hebrews 2,9-11; Mark 10,2-12*) I can't remember whether I told this before, but after God had created Adam and Eve, and they had been in the Garden of Eden for some time, Adam asked God: "God, why did you make Eve so beautiful, so attractive and so desirable?" God answered: "So **you** would love **her**, Adam." Then Adam said: "But why did you make her (you know) so dumb?" And God answered: "So **she**

would love **you**, Adam."

In the story of creation in chapter 1, we are told that with every day of creation, God looked upon what he had made and saw that it was good. When we come to the second chapter, God sees something that was lacking in his creation. He sees Adam surrounded with all these good things he created, but he has no one to share them. So he says: "it is not good for the man to be alone." And so God created Eve from the side of Adam to be a helpmate, one by whom the man would find support and strength and love. The vocabulary the author uses in this passage implies a covenant relationship between the two of them when he writes : "that is why a man "leaves" his father and mother and "clings" to his **wife**, and the two of them become one body." This is the scripture passage Jesus refers to when answering the question that his opponents propose to him in today's gospel.

What a question it is. It is a question that we struggle with in the twenty-first century as much as people struggled with in Jesus' time. The question was: "is it lawful for a husband to divorce his wife?" Let me say first of all, it was not a sincere question, because the Pharisees already assumed they knew the answer. So when Jesus asked: "What did Moses command you," they basically said the answer is "it is lawful because Moses permitted divorce." Jesus' answer was totally unexpected when he said "no, it is not lawful" because it was not God's intention from the beginning. God's intention was that a husband and wife were to be one and a divorce was like cutting a person in two. It's worth noting how Jesus phrased his question: "What did Moses command *you?*" Not, "what did Moses command us?" Jesus is implying that Moses was giving an answer that would accommodate their hard-heartedness.

For all Jewish teachers, divorce was lawful and each

of them had an opinion as to what would justify a divorce – everything from major infidelity to the husband finding a more appealing partner. Jesus threw out all these opinions with his answer - thus alienating himself from Jewish practice and tradition and probably setting almost all of the Jewish teachers against him. There was one other aspect of this question that created a danger for Jesus, which could be why the Pharisees asked him about it. Remember the story of Herod Antipas marrying his brother's wife, Herodias. They both had to get divorced in order to marry each other. John the Baptist condemned their marriage and Herod arrested John and eventually beheaded him. In Jesus' answer about divorce, he is condemning Herod's marriage to Herodias.

You will notice that the real question here is not about divorce, but about divorce and remarriage. Jesus refers to it as adultery. The issue is not just about a man divorcing his wife, which was the only way divorce could happen among the Jews, but in Mark's gospel, Jesus also condemned the Roman custom, which was that a wife could divorce her husband if she chose.

Jesus reminded us of the big picture of what God intended marriage should be. But what happens when that ideal is not always achieved. We know Jesus understood that. So did St. Paul and the early Church. So does the Church today. There are marriages that should never have taken place. There are marriages that for one reason or another do not measure up to the standards of the Church, such as when people are too immature to make a lasting commitment or they are getting married with the wrong intentions. There is not time to go into all the grounds why a marriage is not valid in the eyes of the Church. When that happens, one of the parties can appeal for an annulment. An annulment is not a divorce. A divorce says the marriage no longer exists because one or both parties want to get out. An annulment is an official declaration by those trained in Church law that says the marriage was not valid from the beginning. The Church does not grant divorces. It does grant annulments.

Our Holy Father, just a few weeks ago, issued some new procedures on dealing with annulments. Sometimes it took months or maybe even a year or more to get an annulment. The pope is trying to speed up the process. Some people might still have to wait a long time, but in other cases, there is the possibility of expediting the process. There is no indication that Pope Francis now or in the future plans on making any doctrinal changes; i.e., changing any of the Church's teachings on marriage or divorce, but he is showing a lot more compassion and understanding than we've seen in past years. In addition to speeding up the annulment process, the pope wants to reduce or eliminate any fees as much as possible.

The Holy Father shocked a lot of people last year with his comment: "who am I to judge?" He is not changing the Church's teaching on homosexual relationships. What the pope said is: "if a person is gay and seeks God and has good will, who am I to judge." The Church does not condemn a person because they might be attracted to persons of the same sex. The Church (and the bible) do clearly condemn homosexual activity. Perhaps the Pope means there are too many variables to make a judgment; maybe the pope is saying I can't look into the person's heart and see where he or she is with God. Isn't this true of any act we do? Didn't Jesus say do not judge? A person's behavior can and often deserves to be judged, but only God can look into a person's heart. I do know this much, Francis wants us to know that God is merciful and to know that God's love is infinitely greater than our wickedness. As our Holy Father he doesn't want any of us to be alienated from the Church, our spiritual family, but that we all seek to live as faithful to God as we can and if we fail, we turn to him for mercy. Amen.

28th Sunday in Ordinary Time
October 11, 2015

HOMILY – (*Wisdom 7:7-11; Hebrews 4: 12-13; Mark 10:17-30*) Attitudes toward wealth were ambiguous in the ancient world as well as in Jewish literature. Deuteronomy and some of the Wisdom writings tell us those who obey God's commandments will be rewarded with prosperity. On the other hand, the prophets condemned those who were wealthy for they often took advantage of the poor and had lavish lifestyles without giving consideration to those who were needy. (Jesus' parable of the rich man and Lazarus reflects this attitude.) Our first reading reminds us that there are more precious things in life than having big stashes of wealth. The author of the Book of Wisdom prayed for prudence and the spirit of Wisdom and stated all gold, in view of her (Wisdom), is a little sand, and before her, silver is to be accounted mire (swampy ground or mud). This is very similar to Plato's teaching in the Republic that true riches come with a good and prudent life rather than from the counterfeit treasures of gold.

Perhaps the apostles were thinking of the idea in Deuteronomy that those who obey God's commandments will be rewarded with prosperity. They were surprised to hear Jesus say, "how hard it will be for those who have wealth to enter the kingdom of God." Then Jesus goes on to say that entering the kingdom is not easy for any of us: "Children, how hard it is to enter the kingdom of God." No one knows of any gate in Jerusalem called the "eye of the needle." Jesus' example of a camel getting through the eye of a needle was a graphic way of saying it's not possible. It's only possible with God's grace: "For human beings it is impossible, but not for God. All things are possible for God."

Jesus' response after the rich young man left was in disappointed surprise. He saw that the rich man, whom Jesus saw with love, would prefer worldly wealth to the riches of the kingdom of God. Sometimes those who have some wealth, even a modest amount, feel they are being condemned when they hear today's gospel. Let's realize first of all, practically speaking, the early missionaries, such as St. Paul, would have had great difficulty in founding Churches in various cities and towns without the help of those who were wealthy. The early Churches had to gather somewhere to hear God's word and to celebrate the Eucharist and that was usually at the home of someone of means whose place was large enough to accommodate everyone. Remember church buildings did not exist until the 4th century.

I want to remind you of two other places where Jesus expresses a negative view, or at least a cautious view, of wealth. Jesus said: "where your treasure is there will your heart be." (Mt. 6,21). In that sense, any of us could be led astray by wealth, however much we may have or not have, if we lose our focus on God's kingdom. The other place is where Jesus tells the story of the sower and the seed. Remember the seed that fell among the weeds and as it tried to grow it got choked out. Jesus compared this to those "who hear the word, but the cares of the world, and the lure of wealth, and the desire for other things come in and choke the word and it yields nothing." (Mk.4,19) In that sense, even the poorest among us can be so absorbed by activities and distractions, TV and cell phones and magazines and music and sports and computers, etc., we make no time to pray or come to Church or live as Christ has taught us. That's my homily on the gospel. God has blessed us in many ways. Let us not forget where it comes from.

I want to say a few things personally. The other day I was with a few people and the topic of birthdays came up. I mentioned I was turning 75 on Sunday. One person commented "you're doing pretty good for 75;" and she added with great surprise, "you still drive!" For a split second I worried that maybe I should turn in my car keys. Canon Law requires pastors to write a letter of resignation to the Archbishop when they turn 75. Of course I did, but I added that I would be willing to continue serving here if he wished. Part of the process the Archdiocese has when a pastor turns 75 is for Bishop Binzer to meet with the Parish Pastoral Council, which he did here last week. Next week the Priests' Personnel Board meets and they will make a recommendation to the Archbishop. I feel very sure the Archbishop and the Personnel Board will decide that I stay here.

Other than not having as much energy as I used to, and other than my knees, I would feel in every other way as if I were 20 years younger. My knees keep reminding me though that I'm 75. Several people have asked me if I have Parkinson's when they see my right hand shake. It doesn't always bother me, but I do not have Parkinson's. The doctor said it is just a benign tremor that people sometimes experience only with their right hand. When I go out to eat sometimes, it is embarrassing, and it makes it hard to write legibly, but I could have worse problems. In my early years as a priest I used to enjoy painting and thought I could do a lot more painting when I retired. That's out of the question now (and maybe retirement will be too). I remind myself that Thomas Jefferson started the University of Virginia, secured its location, designed its buildings, planned its curriculum and became its first rector at the age of 76.

I like being here; I like doing what I'm doing most of the time (except when I have three weeks' worth of work that has to be completed in three days). St. Boniface has been good to me and I've tried to return the favor. I'm grateful for all the support I have always been given and the response of our parishioners whenever I've asked for your help. So I'll just say thank you and hope you will keep me in your prayers as I enter into what is laughingly referred to as the "Golden Years." Peace to every one of you.

29th Sunday in Ordinary Time
October 18, 2015

INTRODUCTION – (*Isaiah 53,10-11; Hebrews 4,14-16; Mark 10,35-45*) Today our first reading is a portion of Isaiah's fourth Servant Song. Isaiah tells us God's servant was a mysterious person or persons whose faithfulness and suffering would bring redemption to many people. The four Servant Songs of Isaiah were written 500 years before Christ. This passage was chosen because it corresponds with Jesus' revelation in today's gospel to his apostles that he came to serve and to give his life as a ransom for many. The entire fourth Servant Song is part of the Good Friday service every year.

HOMILY – Jesus and his disciples were fairly near Jerusalem and so Jesus thought he had to warn them about what would happen when they got there. Of course he would teach and heal and cast out demons. Of course he would celebrate the Passover while they were there. But this visit to Jerusalem would be like no other.

He told them he "will be turned over to the chief priests and the scribes, and they will condemn him to death and turn him over to the Gentiles and they will mock him and spit on him and scourge him and kill him; and after three days he will arise." The disciples knew he had many enemies, so it's no wonder St. Mark tells us "they were astonished and those following him were afraid." (*Mk. 10,12*) We are astonished too, when we hear what comes next, which is the beginning of today's gospel.

James and John, members of Jesus' inner group (Peter, James and John) asked Jesus for a favor. They wanted the highest and most important position in Jesus kingdom, after Jesus himself. An interesting little detail here is that Matthew, in his gospel, tells us, the mother of James and John asked for this favor. Was Matthew trying to make James and John not look so crass, or did she also join in with her sons in making this request? Little did they know that when Jesus would enter into his kingdom, there would be two thieves, hanging on two crosses, one on his right and one on his left. Jesus told James and John, they didn't know what they were asking. Were they ready to suffer for having followed the Lord (that's what "drinking the cup or being baptized (i.e. dunked) in the water in which Jesus was to be baptized." They said they could, and Jesus promised them they would. But he could not offer them the status and position they were asking for.

Again, as we heard just one month ago, Jesus knew they had no idea of what he was talking about when he warned them of his suffering and death. Their thoughts were on an earthly kingdom where they would share fame and fortune, while the kingdom he was speaking about was with the Father in heaven and the road that led to God's heavenly kingdom involved a life of commitment and fidelity to Christ, even perhaps having to lay down one's life for him. They had yet to learn that lesson.

So Jesus did not get angry – he answered gently: "you do not know what you are asking." Is this where we sometimes go wrong in our prayers, asking for something that we don't yet understand will only get in the way of our serving our God. Maybe we're looking and praying for something that we think will lift us up above most other people, especially people who have tended to put us down, or maybe we're greedily looking for more material things, or hoping to see our enemies experience some bad effect for the way they've hurt us. Maybe we are envious of those we work with or study with and we wish we were as smart as they, or maybe we pray for greater peace in our own family, wishing to be like the Jones who are looking as us and who are wishing they had such a happy family life as our family seems to enjoy.

There's a lesson to be learned here. When we see in today's gospel the apostles following Jesus, dreaming of the glorious worldly status they soon will enjoy, begrudging some of their fellow apostles getting a few steps higher on the social ladder than they might achieve, at least they didn't walk away from Jesus. They had enough faith and trust to believe that he was the one they had to follow, even when he said "no" – not even to them but to their mothers who were pleading for them. That's the trouble, I think, with many people's spiritual lives today. They pray. They don't get what they want. They may pray again and even get their mother and maybe other friends and relatives involved in interceding for them and Jesus doesn't seem to hear their request. So they drift away – away from the one who loves them most and the one who calls them to true greatness as he tells us: whoever among you who wants to be great shall be your servant.

Sometimes we don't know what we're asking, but Jesus said "keep on asking, keep on knocking." And don't give up on Jesus for faithfully following him will allow him to keep teaching us.

30th Sunday in Ordinary Time
October 25, 2015

INTRODUCTION – (*Jeremiah 31:7-9; Hebrews 5:1-6; Mark 10:46-52*) Today's first reading is a short excerpt from a major part of the Book of Jeremiah. Jeremiah lived during the time of the Babylonian exile, (roughly 600 years before Christ) and much of the time he was prophesizing doom and gloom. But in today's passage his message provides hope for the exiles, assuring them that God would bring them back to their own land. It is in this section of the Book of Jeremiah that God promises he would raise up King David for them and he would make a new covenant with his people. Today's passage has been chosen because of the mention that God would bring back to their land even the blind and the lame. The passage prepares us for today's gospel where Jesus, Son of David, gives sight to a blind man.

HOMILY – Two pirates, Morty and Sol, meet in a bar. Sol has a patch over one eye, a hook for a hand and a wooden peg leg. "Ye gads, matey," says Monty. What happened to ya?" Sol says, "Me ship was attacked, and a cannonball lopped off me leg. So now I got me a wooden peg." "And yer hand?" asks Marty. "When me ship sank, a shark bit me hand off. So now I got me a hook." OK, but what's with the eye patch?" "I got a piece of dirt in me eye, and now I'm blind in that eye." "But a person don't go blind from a tiny piece of dirt." "True," says Sol, "but it was me first day with the hook." (*Reader's Digest, Nov. 2015, pg. 74*)

There are many forms of blindness. It may be physical blindness when our eyes cannot see any more; but it could be blindness in our mind such as the inability to see someone else's point of view, someone's need, or someone's hurt. When someone who had been blind can suddenly see, it is wonderful. People who get cataract surgery experience that. One of the joys I had as a teacher was when one of my students grasped a point I was trying to make. Suddenly it was as if they came out of the dark; they saw the light and their face lit up with that "ah-ha" experience. What I have to say today may not create an "ah-ha" experience; you might think "I've heard all of that before;" but even then, it's worth being reminded of the points our gospel makes.

A couple of points are obvious: (1) perseverance in prayer, a theme that Jesus spoke of more than once. Bartimaeus would not give up calling out to Jesus for his help; even when everyone around him was trying their best to get him to keep quiet. (2) A second obvious point is that after meeting Jesus, Bartimaeus followed Jesus "on the way." He didn't just say thanks for the healing, Jesus, and go away. Sometimes we do that when we pray. After God gives us what we ask for, we move him to the bottom of our list of priorities until we need something else from him. Bartimaeus didn't do that. He followed Jesus. Since Mark gives us the name "Bartimaeus," (*most times recipients of miracles are not named*), I wonder if this is an indication that, in a short time, he became well-known among the disciples and was one of Jesus' faithful followers.

I would like to say a little more about Jericho where this event took place. It is about 15 miles from Jerusalem and about 9 or 10 miles from the Dead Sea. Archeologists believe it is the oldest town on earth with a massive defense wall which goes back about nine thousand years before Christ. It is also the lowest city on earth, 850 feet below sea level. (Our death valley out west is about 280 feet below sea level). Since Jerusalem is 2500 feet above sea level, getting from Jericho to Jerusalem (a 15-mile climb), which the disciples were getting ready to do, would be quite a chore. Perhaps this climb could be symbolic of the ordeal Jesus was soon to face. Mark tells us Bartimaeus went along with Jesus as he followed him "on the way."

A last detail I'm sure Mark wants us to note is that although Bartimaeus was blind, he had more insight into who Jesus was than Jesus' disciples who had been with Jesus for three years. Bartimaeus called Jesus "Son of David." In those days, that was a political term, indicating the Messiah, the descendant of King David who would be the savior of God's people. Only Peter, up to this point in the gospel, was the only human person who acknowledged Jesus as the Messiah. It's also worth noting that the cry of Bartimaeus is what we pray every time we begin Mass ("Jesus, have pity on me." – In Greek it is: Ἰησοῦ, ἐλέησόν). "Christ, have mercy," the Greek is Χριστέ, ἐλέησόν. Does it sound familiar?

In this miracle story, St. Mark is revealing Jesus to us and is encouraging us to choose Jesus as our leader and to follow his way – the way that leads to life.

All Saints
November 1, 2015

INTRODUCTION – (*Revelation 7,2-4.9-14; I John 3,1-3; Matthew 5,1-12a*) In its four and a half billion years our planet has seen an overwhelming number of catastrophes. Somehow, under God's creative hand, planet earth continues to survive and even thrive. We have however, through our brilliance, discovered ways to annihilate all of creation if we are not wise and prudent. In considering some of the catastrophes the world may yet experience, The Book of Revelation, asks a critical question: "who can survive?"

Today's first reading is the answer to that question. Those who survive are too many to count. In giving us the number 144,000, we are dealing with a symbolic number. It is the number that represents completion. 12 months brings our year to completion. 12 is the number of all of the tribes of Israel. There were 12 apostles. 12 x 12 x 1000 symbolized the completed number of all God's people, none would be left out. People from every race, every land and every language are among those who will survive, and as I said, they are too many to be counted. The key to survival is to follow Christ faithfully and in doing so we will share in Christ's victory over death and enjoy the blessing of eternal happiness forever.

HOMILY – Today's feast of All Saints began around the time that Constantine became converted to Christ – the early fourth century. In those days, there was no formal process for declaring a person a saint. It was just a matter of the Christian community remembering and commemorating a holy person as one who is surely in heaven after they passed away. Those who were martyrs, who gave their life for Christ, were the first to be honored and recognized as saints. And that's how this feast began; its intent was to honor all the martyrs. As time went on, those who lived lives of outstanding virtue were recognized as models of Christian holiness and were honored as such. The Christian Community, often with the approval or leadership of the bishop, continued to give such recognition of holiness to individuals. It wasn't until the year 973 when the first papal canonization occurred. The lengthy process now required to prove extraordinary sanctity took form in the last 500 years.

I could mention many, many holy people whom the Church honors such as our Blessed Mother, St. Boniface, St. Patrick, St. Augustine, St. Jerome, St. Lawrence, St. Thomas More (a man for all seasons), St. Francis of Assisi, St. Anthony, St. Teresa, St. Catherine of Sienna, St. Francis Xavier, etc. You might be interested in knowing some of the new names that have been added to this list in recent years. Pope John Paul added 110 new names, mostly people we've never heard of although we may have heard of St. Maximillian Kolbe, St. Rose Philippine Duchesne, and St. Padre Pio. Benedict XVI added 45 new saints including two people who lived in the New York territory: St. Kateri Tekakwitha, St. Marianne Cope who eventually dedicated herself to serving those who had leprosy in Hawaii; his list also includes St. Damien who lived with and worked with the lepers, Jeanne Jugan who started the Little Sisters of the Poor, St. Andre Bessette of Montreal Canada and St. Hildegard of Bingen. Pope Francis started off canonizing a group of 812 Italian martyrs who refused to convert from Christianity to Islam after the Muslims took over their town in 1480. Francis also canonized 26 other individuals including Pope John XXIII, Pope John Paul II, Junipero Serra, and most recently on Oct 18, Louis and Zelie Martin (the parents of St. Therese – aka the Little Flower whose statue we have).

Why so many saints? Do they need to be honored? St. Bernard says our devotion does not add the slightest thing to what is theirs. They have no need of honor from us. Clearly, if we venerate their memory, it serves us, not them. Their lives assure us that holiness is possible, they teach us by their lives and their writing how to serve God, and they can intercede for us when we need God's help. I can never understand people who argue against praying to the saints. They are the very same people who, I am sure, ask their friends to pray for them when they are desperate. Why not ask God's friends to pray for you.

Today's feast honors not only the famous individuals who have served God in a heroic way, but it also honors millions of others who have tried to live a good and holy life, including those who have fallen down along the way, but who have gotten up and kept on going. St. Paul so often in his letters refers to the people he was writing to, the people he was serving or had served as saints. The word saint means holy, and if we do the best we can to love and serve God – that makes us a saint even here on earth. The saints that we officially call "saint" are many, but the rest of us are in that big crowd of people we heard about in the first reading, a multitude which no one could number. That gives me great confidence and hope. So, happy feast day, everyone. Amen.

31st Sunday in Ordinary Time
November 5, 2006

HOMILY – (*Deuteronomy 6:2-6; Hebrews 7:23-28; Mark 12:28b-34*) The rabbis and Jewish religious leaders at the time of Jesus would often discuss which of their 613 laws was the most important. They asked Jesus' opinion and as usual Jesus got right to the heart of the matter. Jesus was not saying the others do not count or are unimportant. He was saying that love is the spirit behind all of them. If we follow the command of love, we will keep the others, if we keep the others without love we are legalists or as Paul says in his famous 13th chapter of 1 Corinthians "If I have not love, I am nothing." Jesus was asked for one commandment, but he gave us two, to show that the two are inseparable. Part of the problems people have in today's world is that they have forgotten the first part of this commandment. That's why they have problems with the second. It's interesting too to notice the word "commandment." It reminds us that we don't always feel love for God or for others, but we are obliged to do it anyway if we are going to fulfill our highest potential as a human being and if we are going to please God. I was going to bring with me today all the books I have that have the word "love" in the title. But there were too many to bring. So, just think of a big stack of books up here. My purpose in mentioning there are so many books is to illustrate that love can be very complex and learning to love God and others is not always as easy as we would like to think that it is. It is interesting that the English language, which has a plentitude of words, relies so heavily on the one word "love" to mean so many things. Even the Greek language, which was rather primitive, had three words for the word love, depending on the kind of love that was being spoken of. We use the one word "love" to describe everything from a score in tennis to the most selfish, lustful cravings to the most sublime and unselfish act of kindness toward another. For this reason it is a challenge to talk about and a challenge to put into practice.

The biggest misconception about love in today's world is to equate it with feelings. Too many people think love means having nice warm, friendly feelings toward someone. Well, it is and it isn't. Love is an emotion, but the kind of love Jesus is talking about is much more. Warm feelings don't always feed the hungry or help a person in need. Love is not primarily something vague, fuzzy and warm. Love is a matter of what one does rather than what one feels. One of the Peanuts' cartoons had Linus telling his sister Lucy that he wanted to be a doctor when he grew up. Lucy responded in her usual cynical fashion by saying "You, a doctor? That's a laugh. You know why you couldn't be a doctor? Because you don't love humankind." Linus thought about this for a moment then said "I do love humankind. It's people I can't stand." It's easy to have nice warm, happy feelings of love for vague humanity, or even for a God who will do for us whatever we want him to do. But where are those nice warm happy feelings when a parent has to get up in the middle of the night to care for a crying baby or when an adult child has to care for an aging parent or even when God commands things we don't want to do. When we do the right thing, that's love at work also. There is a beautiful story in Chicken Soup for the Soul about a little girl who was dying of a very rare disease. Her only hope for survival was to get a blood transfusion from her five year old brother who had survived the same disease and whose body had developed antibodies needed to combat the illness. The doctor explained to the little boy what a transfusion was and asked if he would be willing to give blood to his sister. He hesitated for a moment then said "yes, if it will save Lisa." As the transfusion progressed he lay in bed next to his sister and smiled, along with all the medical staff, as they saw color return to Lisa's cheeks. Then the little boy's smile faded and with a very serious look on his face and a trembling voice he asked the doctor "Will I start to die now?" The boy had mis-understood the doctor and thought he would have to give his sister all his blood. Love is not always a happy, painless, easy, carefree thing. Love, when it is real love, requires unselfishness and that's not always easy, especially when it is required of us over long periods of time.

Love has some difficult elements to it such as sacrifice and unselfishness. You know, when we are born we're pretty self-centered creatures. We know when we're hungry, when we're in pain, when we're tired and we don't mind letting the whole world know about it. That's OK for a baby. But we're supposed to grow out of that stage and realize we're not the center of the universe. When we grow in love we are learning to reach out to others and this is a sign of maturity. A word about love for God. Feelings enter in here too and when they're not present people become confused. When they don't get good feelings from prayer or Mass they often feel they are losing their faith or God has abandoned them or they just quit trying. Sometimes our love for God produces good feelings, but love for God is not measured by how we feel. Basically, love for God is a matter of giving God our trust, our time and our obedience. Jesus gave us a reliable measure of our love for God when he told us: "If you love me you will keep my commandments."

We come together today to offer God our worship and our love. As we recall Jesus unselfish love for us in giving his life for us on the cross, we ask him to help us learn the true meaning of love. Amen.

32nd Sunday in Ordinary Time
November 9, 2015

INTRODUCTION – (*1 Kings 17,10-16; Hebrews 9,24-28; Mark 12,38-44*) Our first reading will make more sense if we know that the events described in the reading happened during a severe famine. We have to marvel at the faith of the widow in our first reading, a faith that is reflected in the offering of another poor widow in the gospel.

HOMILY – It is required by the bishop that once a year pastors give a financial report to the parish and I thought, because of today's gospel, this would be a good time to do so. Our fiscal year ends on June 30, so these two reports (one for the parish and one for the school) tell us what was budgeted from July 1, 2014, to June 30, 2015 (first column), what were our actual income and expenses for that period of time (second column) and our budget for the current year: July 1, 2015, to June 30, 2016 (third column). If you look at the yellow paper, center column, where you find the actual figures for last year, you will see the parish did well: $46,852 ahead for the fiscal year 2014/2015. Sunday contributions (line item #1) were pretty much what we expected, (for which I thank all of you). But besides Sunday contributions, what really put us over the top were bequests (line # 4) and special gifts (line # 8). Expenses were held pretty much in line, except for salaries (line # 18), which increased due to the unexpected loss of Fr. Lammeier who helped us a lot, both financially and in other ways. Another expense was a part time maintenance person we needed to catch up on some of the work we were getting behind on. A third item that went beyond our expectations was Capital Improvements (item # 36) which involved replacing a lot of deteriorating walkways and getting a good used piano which was offered to us at too good of a deal to pass up. So much for the last fiscal year which is all ancient history now. By the way, I am not going to mention all the line items. I'm just mentioning a few that might jump out at you. As to our current year, we are running in the red (only the budgeted figures for our current year are on that sheet in the third column). For the current year, our Sunday collections are $9000 less that what our budget calls for and bequests and special gifts are $ 85,000 less that what we budgeted. That's not happy news. If anyone has been watching, they may have observed that our attendance has been dropping off, which I can only attribute to the fact that our congregation is aging. This, of course, is going to impact our revenue. We are in the process of reaching out to new homeowners in Northside and inviting them to come to St. Boniface.

Now as regards the school, the finance report is printed on the light grey paper. We ended the last fiscal year in the black. Again, gifts and bequests helped put us over the top. Salaries and benefits are our biggest expense, of course. You might be confused by item # 24 where we budgeted a large amount for maintenance. That was because we needed a new roof over the gym, but we were able to pay for it in the previous fiscal year so the actual payment for the roof had been made before the fiscal year began. The school report includes our pre-school, which is turning out to be a bigger expense than we had planned on. If you have questions about any of this, Jenni, our business manager would be happy to answer them for you.

In our gospel Jesus, who could read people's minds and hearts, commented on the humility of a lady who gave a tiny donation to the Temple and the pride of those who made big donations. If a person gives a small donation and it is made with love, they should not be ashamed; if they can give a large amount, they should be grateful that they are in such a position as to be able to do so. Not being Jesus and not being able to read hearts, I can only assume that a lot of love comes with every donation, but as I am the one who has to pay the bills, I do need to say that those who can afford to make a significant donation do help us pay all our bills. Asking for money is not my favorite pastime, but it is my responsibility to inform you that the church you love is coming up short so far this year. I'm glad I could get this message in before Christmas. Perhaps it might help us to do a little better in our Christmas collection. I thank you for patiently listening, and I thank you for whatever you can do to keep our parish operating in the black.

33rd Sunday in Ordinary Time
November 15, 2015

INTRODUCTION – (*Daniel 12,1-3; Hebrews 10,11-14; Mark 13,24-32*) Most of us, I am sure, are familiar with the last book of the Bible, the Book of Revelation. Because the entire New Testament was originally written in Greek, and the Book of Revelation began with the Greek word "apocalypsis," a word which means revelation, the book is also referred to as the Apocalypse. What most people do not know is there are a number of other sections of the Bible that are apocalyptic in nature; that is, they reveal to God's people what is going to take place. Usually they were composed during a time when God's people were being persecuted to give hope to God's people during those difficult times. The message usually was that if God's people remained faithful to God, their sufferings would soon be at an end and God, or perhaps God's delegate, the Messiah, would overcome God's enemies and would initiate an era of peace. This era of peace was spoken as God's reign or God's kingdom. Our first reading today, from the Book of Daniel, written about 165 BC, is an example of apocalyptic writing. The Jews were being forced to adopt the pagan religion of the Greeks, otherwise they were persecuted and killed. The time was described as "unsurpassed in distress." In today's passage, Daniel the seer predicts that soon the Archangel Michael, the guardian of the Jews, would come to the aid of God's people. The passage contains a clear belief in resur- rection to glory for those who remained faithful and a resurrection to everlasting horror for those who had not.

HOMILY – For those who like to use big words, I have one for you: eschatology. It means a study of the last things. It derives from the Greek eschaton – the things that are to take place at the end of the world. As the year draws to a close, our scripture readings want us to remember that our world as we know it will not continue on forever. God has other plans for us – to be with him forever. It is basic common sense, if we are aware of what is ahead, we will be better prepared to deal with it when it comes.

We just heard a little bit of what the Bible teaches us about the end time, the eschaton. Prior to today's reading, Mark tells us the topic came up as the apostles were admiring the Temple. Jesus prophesied its destruction (which was to take place in the year 70 AD); then he began speaking of wars and natural disasters and families breaking apart and other tribulations that his people would suffer. Then we come to today's gospel. The central feature of the end time will be the return of the glorified Jesus and his calling together those who have lived as God has desired we should. Today's first reading, taken from the Book of Daniel, said they will live forever. Daniel doesn't say what will happen to the others who have not followed God's ways, but it isn't pretty.

Let me repeat that Jesus' return is the key feature of the end time. In today's gospel, Jesus is telling us that the whole cosmos will signal his coming. The sun and moon and stars will no longer be needed, for Christ himself will be our light. Just as we know that summer is coming from signs in nature, so there will be signs that the Son of Man is coming soon. Just how soon is the big question. It is vague enough to urge us to always be ready to meet the

Lord. That's a message that bears repeating, and so Jesus repeats this message in a second parable a few verses after today's gospel when he compares the coming of the Son of Man to a man who goes on a long journey. His servants do not know when he might return, whether in the evening or midnight or early morning or whenever, and he warns his servants that when he returns he doesn't want to find them goofing off. It is a parable that exhorts us to constant vigilance.

Almost always, Jesus refers to himself as the Son of Man. It is an ambiguous title and Jesus probably uses it to make people think deeply about what it might mean. No one (none of the apostles or anyone) used this title to refer to Jesus, except Jesus himself. Basically it means "a human being," but there is a passage in the Book of Daniel (not today's passage) which describes one like a "Son of Man" who comes on the clouds of heaven and who is presented to God (referred to as "the Ancient One") who gives this Son of Man authority, honor and royal power over all the nations of the world so people of every race and nation and language would obey him. It is obvious that this second meaning far surpasses the idea of just "a human being."

There are a couple of things in today's gospel that really challenge Scripture scholars. Jesus said "this generation will not pass away until all these things have taken place." Some scholars interpret "this generation" to mean the Jewish people, or Christians or the human race in general. Others say it refers to the destruction of Jerusalem and the Temple; i.e., the signs that will announce Jesus' coming. It certainly reflects the immanence of his coming, perhaps it refers to his coming to each one of us at the time of our death.

Another challenge for scholars is Jesus' statement about when he shall return. He says: "of that day or hour, no one knows, neither the angels in heaven nor the Son, but only the Father." It could refer to his human nature, which had to grow in wisdom and age and grace just as we do, and his human nature was not informed of the day nor the hour. Some scholar refer to the words "nor the Son" as an addition by a scribe. Nowhere else in Mark's gospel does Jesus refer to himself as simply "the Son." As a matter of fact, in the *Acts of the Apostles* (1,7), Jesus said to the apostles "it is not for you [disciples] to know the times or periods." He does not say "it is not for me to know," but he says "it is not for you to know." There is no conclusive understanding; maybe he did know and wouldn't say, or maybe he didn't know because of his human limitations.

100% of those who have predicted the second coming of Christ and the end of the world at a certain day and time have been wrong. Just two weeks ago, I got a warning by email that it will happen before the end of the year. If they are right, they would be the first person in 2000 years who was. How do we live in this period of expectation of Christ's second coming? Some people expect it's right around the corner. Some think, "oh, we have to hear about that again. It probably won't happen for a million years." While others are too busy to think about any of this stuff right now and they have forgotten that Jesus wants us to live in expectation of his return, so when he comes we can meet him not as a stranger but as a friend.

Christ the King
November 22, 2015

INTRODUCTION – *(Daniel 7:13-14; Revelation 1:5-8; John 18:33-37)* Our first reading is a very short reading. It would be difficult to understand without knowing what immediately preceded it. So, I'll tell you. One night Daniel had a vision or a dream of a great sea full of monsters. Out of the water came four beasts; the first like a lion with eagle's wings. It could stand on two feet and had a human mind. The second was like a bear with three tusks; the third like a leopard with four wings and four heads; and the fourth was beyond description having great iron teeth and ten horns along with a little horn with human eyes. The monsters represented nations that had subjected the Jews to extreme suffering: the Babylonians (today's Iraq), the Medes (today's Iran), the Persians (also today's Iran) and lastly the Greeks. That was a summary of the first part of Daniel's vision. But in spite of all the suffering, there is hope, hope that God will send someone to save his people from all their suffering. This will give us a taste of apocalyptic writing – writing that stresses the element of hope for those who remain faithful to God. The rest of Daniel's vision is the part that stresses hope and salvation for God's people. One like a son of man comes on the scene and is presented before God (the Ancient One) and this son of man is given dominion and power over all of creation. The person Daniel describes as coming on the clouds of heaven is not just "a" son of man but "the" son of man, the savior whom God will send who will establish a kingdom that will last forever.

In the gospel for today we see this Son of Man Daniel saw in his vision standing before Pilate trying to explain his kingdom to Pilate. For one reason or another, Pilate didn't want to listen and so in a still famous line: "what is truth," Pilate abruptly ends the conversation and leaves the room where they had been talking.

HOMILY – Each of the four gospels offers its own unique perspective on Jesus' passion and death. In John's gospel, the dominant part of his account of Jesus' passion is the trial before Pilate. A short segment of the trial between Pilate and Jesus is today's gospel. Pilate has Jesus alone in a court room in his residence (called a praetorium). The Jewish priests and elders who wanted Pilate to execute Jesus were outside. Pilate found himself going back and forth during this trial. Pilate, as a representative of the Roman Emperor, has the task of finding out if Jesus is a king for he would then be a rebel against the Emperor, Tiberius Caesar. Jesus' answers focus less on himself being king and more on his kingdom, which is not of this world.

When Pilate asked "are you the king of the Jews," Jesus answered "do you say this on your own, or have others told you about me?" I always wondered why Jesus asked this question. I am guessing perhaps Jesus is questioning whether he has the freedom to speak openly to Pilate or if Pilate's mind is already full of the charges his enemies have brought against Jesus. It's not that Jesus didn't know what was being said about him. He could read minds and hearts. I am just supposing that Jesus wanted Pilate to be aware as to whether Pilate was just working with what he's heard ("hearsay") or whether he had an open mind. Pilate reacted negatively: "Am I a Jew?" he asks, as if to say "do you think I would give two cents for what any of them think?" It was common knowledge that Pilate had deep hatred for the Jews and vice-versa. So Pilate, still in the dark about Jesus, asks: "What have you done?" Jesus takes this as an opportunity to speak openly and honestly. Jesus talked about the kind of kingdom he ruled, a kingdom built on truth. This is why he came into this world, to give witness to the truth. I suppose by now, Pilate was beginning to feel as if he was the one on trial. It was clear to Pilate that Jesus had done nothing wrong and Jesus is pressing him to accept this truth (Pilate had a hard time understanding "truth" whatever it was), while he was struggling with a lot of pressure on him from the crowd outside to put Jesus to death. Besides, a person's life wasn't all that important to Pilate (or to most of the Romans for that matter). He actually lost his job as governor, fired by his boss in Rome, because of his brutality toward the Jews. So with this background, perhaps we can understand why Pilate walked out on Jesus saying "what is truth?"

On this feast of Christ the King, we are prompted to ask ourselves if Jesus is really king in our hearts. Does he really rule our lives? Is he king for us on Sunday (if even that much), while we make up our own rules the rest of the week. The pressures of life sometimes lead us to walk away rather than keep our mind and heart open to his word. If we fail, however, God in his great mercy is always there, ready to help us serve and love him better. Amen.

Rosella Robinson Funeral
November 12, 2005

HOMILY – In Rosella we have all had a good friend. Offering sympathy is in order, because we've lost a step-mother, a grandmother, an aunt, a friend, a wonderful lady. At the same time we are not here to grieve but to celebrate. We celebrate that Rosella lived a good and full life for 95 years, that she died a peaceful death, that she lived and died filled with God's grace. We also celebrate our faith that she is now enjoying the rewards of eternal life. As our first reading says: "The souls of the just are in the hand of God, and no torment shall touch them. They seemed in the view of the foolish to be dead...but they are in peace." For the bible, a fool is someone who doesn't believe in God. Their vision of reality is limited. Their mind is closed to anything they cannot discover for themselves. So death is the end of life in the view of a foolish person, since they have no belief in God. But for one who has faith, there is more to life than just the few years we spend on this earth. There is unending life with God. If a fool is someone who doesn't believe in God, then by those standards, Rosella was a person with profound and extraordinary wisdom. Her life was centered on God and her prayers were for those she loved that they too would live a life centered on God.

I was talking with George the other evening and he said whenever she called him she would introduce herself as: "This is Rosella, your godmother." She took her role seriously. George said by reminding him she was his godmother, he thinks she was also reminding him that she had the responsibility and the authority to straighten him out if he needed it. I'm sure all her godchildren got gentle reminders at times and I'm sure they got lots of extra prayers as well.

The gospel I chose for our Mass today was on the Eucharist. The Eucharist was so important to Rosella. She would come to Mass every day when she could. Jesus tells us "Whoever eats my flesh and drinks my blood has eternal life, and I will raise him on the last day." It is in this faith that I can say we are here to celebrate, knowing Rosella was well nourished with the bread of life, the body and blood of Jesus who promised: "whoever eats this bread will live forever."

In 1952 our mother, Alice, died. Rosella knew Alice and often Rosella told me that because of the friendship they shared, she felt she should step in and help out after Alice died. And she did when she married my father in February, 1953. For over 52 years she has been with us. She was a caregiver through and through. When she was finished caring for us, she cared for her sister, Catherine, and she cared for her grandchildren. It was what made her happy, to be needed by someone. And she didn't want to inconvenience anyone. She would always tell me, "Now if you have something planned and something happens to me, don't change your plans. Just go ahead with what you were going to do."

All kinds of great things could be said about Rosella, her kindness, her gentleness, her faith, her dedication to family. One thing I always remarked about was that I seldom heard her say a negative thing about anyone. Dad would often get frustrated with her when he wanted to complain about someone and she would make excuses for them or stand up for them.

I have no worries about where she is now. I'm sure she can say with St. Paul: "I have fought the good fight, I have finished the race, I have kept the faith. From now on a merited crown awaits me..." I believe she now must have a double crown, the first for living with my father (I loved my father, but those who knew him will understand what I mean). The second crown would be for taking over the care of five children, four in grade school and me in high school.

Since she's been at the Little Sisters, who took wonderful care of her, I would try to visit her every week. Whenever I was about to leave she would say "If I don't see you next week, I'll be on my way to heaven." She was peaceful with her God, with herself and with those who knew her. She was ready to go. So I can't grieve. I can only say thank you God for giving us a good woman to take care of us when we needed her, a good woman to inspire us in the way of holiness and a good woman to pray for us and whom I am sure will continue to pray for us until we're all together.

When she died a week ago we were enjoying the beautiful colors of fall. The red and yellow and gold trees were telling us that summer is over. But we do not grieve that the green leaves are gone and that nature is shutting down for we know it's only temporary. Spring will return and so will a new life for Rosella and for all of us, a life that will never end. Amen.

Third Sunday of Easter
May 8, 2011

Delivered at the 50th Wedding Anniversary Mass at St. Peter in Chains Cathedral

HOMILY – (Acts 2:14, 22-33; 1 Peter 1:17-21; Luke 24:13-35) I am honored to celebrate with you today. I'm Fr. Joe Robinson, pastor of St. Boniface Church. I am also the dean of the Cathedral Deanery and it was because I am dean that I originally thought that's why I was invited to preside at today's liturgy. But the idea did cross my mind that since I have been ordained for 47 years, maybe I was asked to come because I'm about as old as everyone else here. That way you all would feel more comfortable. Maybe with a little luck and God's blessing, I'll make it to my 50th anniversary in a few years. A 50th anniversary is something worth celebrating and something worth giving thanks for that is what we are doing here today.

I have three little stories you might enjoy (all three are from *Reader's Digest: Laughter, the Best Medicine*, pgs. 154, 163 & 175): 1) A lady was telling her friend that after she and her husband had a huge argument, they ended up not talking to each other. Finally, on the third day, he asked where one of his shirts was. "Oh," she said, "now you are speaking to me." He was confused and asked: "What are you talking about?" "Haven't you noticed I haven't spoken to you for three days?" she asked. "No," he said. "I just thought we were getting along."

2) A lady and her sister in law were discussing how long they've been married. The sister-in-law commented: "you've been married to my brother for 50 years. That's a long time." "A long, long time" she agreed. Then she smiled and said: "you know the strangest idea occurred to me the other day. If I had killed your brother the first time I felt like it, I'd be out of jail by now."

3) A husband and wife were comparing notes one day. She pointed out to him, "I have a higher IQ, did better on my SAT's and made more money than you." "Yeah," he said. "But when you look at the big picture, I'm still way ahead of you." Puzzled she asked: "How do you figure?" "I married better," he replied.

So, in the name of the Church, in the name of the sacredness of the sacrament of marriage, I thank you for your 50 years of dedication and love for each other. I thank you for doing more than just silently getting along and for not killing one another when you felt like it. I hope today that you each feel deep in your heart that you got the better part of the deal when you got married.

Leonard Pitts, whose editorials appear in the Enquirer, wrote one a week ago that was inspired by the marriage of Prince William and Kate Middleton. I am going to steal some of his ideas, ideas that are profound, ideas that will not surprise any of you but are always worth remembering. He said marriage is an act of faith.

It is a willingness to make a bet that it's possible to love someone always and forever. As you all know, loving each other always and forever is not just romance. It is as much a function of commitment and work as it is a function of love. The capacity and willingness to make that bet, to put in the required work, to be faithful to a commitment, are slowly disappearing from American life. Fifty years ago 70 percent of all American adults were married. Now it's about 54 percent. As so many marriages end in disaster, for a numerous reasons, marriage in this day and age is an act of hope as well as an act of faith. It is an act of defiance against cynicism and pessimism. St. Paul has given us one of the best descriptions there is of love when he tells us its patient and kind, it is not jealous or snobbish or rude or self-seeking, not prone to anger or holding grudges. There is no limit to its forbearance, its trust, its hope, its power to endure. If people have that kind of love, no wonder Paul can say, "love never fails."

Our gospel today presents us with the picture of Jesus' frightened and frustrated disciples. This wasn't the first time they were frightened or frustrated by our Lord nor was it the last time. The kingdom he came to offer would be much greater than they were capable of imagining. The way into that kingdom would be the cross. Through good times and bad, he never abandoned them even when they deserted him. In our journey through life sometimes things can get pretty discouraging. Things don't always happen the way we think they should and we feel anger, discouragement and sadness. Through good times and bad, our Lord is with us, although we do not always recognize him. He has won victory for us over all those forces that seek to pull us down. He has declared victory even over our ultimate enemy - sin and death. It is that victory that we celebrate especially during this Easter season. All through the year Jesus is with us, teaching us with his word in the Scriptures and nourishing us with the bread of his own flesh and blood as he does today.

Again I congratulate you and thank you for overcoming the challenges and fears and discouragements we all face at times throughout our lives. I congratulate you and thank you for your patience, your many sacrifices, your sensitivity to one another, your care and concern, your enduring love. May you trust in our Lord's presence with you and always experience hope and joy and a love that never fails. Amen.

From Rita Robinson Ring, Co-founder of Shepherds of Christ

God has chosen us, we are to turn to Christ with greater generosity, and as baptized Christians to grow in our knowing and loving capacity.

God has put His handprint on us in baptism giving to us the virtues of faith, hope and love. These are theological virtues. We must pray to God for the increase in these virtues and we respond to the grace He outpours to us. In praying for the increase in faith we can see more and more the vision of the Heavenly Father. We can hope for our eternal salvation and help spread that hope in our lives to others and we can share more deeply in God's loving activity – loving more supernaturally as we cooperate by responding to the gifts given by God of greater faith, hope and love.

God is with us, God wants us to spread the good news, to turn toward Him in loving union performing good acts according to His will.

Fr. Joe's book teaches us about love and life in God. Fr. Joe's book teaches us about the gift of the Mass and the Church, and about salvation history. We live more every day according to the scriptures in peace, love and joy. We know Jesus, we love Him. He is operating in us.

We all seek happiness – Happiness is found in God –

In reading the weekly scriptures and reading Fr. Joe's homily – God's loving self-communication to us will grow in our lives – as we respond in love to Him.

This book and the scripture come alive in our lives every Sunday after we read the scriptures and Fr. Joe's homily before Mass.

God communicates His own life through grace and man in return gives himself to God and his fellowman in loving service.

Happiness comes to us in dying to those ways not likened to God and rising in the spiritual life in that image and likeness of Christ.

We love Fr. Joe's jokes that help us to clear our minds and laugh and listen.

He told me of a little boy who was drawing a picture in art class and the teacher said "Who is this?" And the little boy said, "It is God."

The teacher said, "Nobody knows what God looks like." The little boy said, "When I get done – they will know."

In baptism we have been given a sharing in God's life with this elevated knowing and loving capacity.

It is up to us to pray to God for the grace to grow to know and love Him more – to be more and more likened to God.

In the pages of Fr. Joe's homilies we learn more and more about God, about loving God and loving others as ourselves – God is love – God is the source of love – We are to Respond to God's love.

Excerpt from *Response to God's Love* by Fr. Edward Carter, S.J.

"... In reference to Christianity, God himself is the ultimate mystery. Radically, God is completely other and transcendent, hidden from man in his inner life, unless he chooses to reveal himself. Let us briefly look at this inner life of God.

The Father, in a perfect act of self-expression, in a perfect act of knowing, generates his son. The

Son, the Word, is, then, the immanent expression of God's fullness, the reflection of the Father. Likewise, from all eternity, the Father and the Son bring forth the Holy Spirit in a perfect act of loving.

At the destined moment in human history, God's self-expression, the Word, immersed himself into man's world. God's inner self-expression now had also become God's outer self-expression. Consequently, the mystery of God becomes the mystery of Christ. In Christ, God tells us about himself, about his inner life, about his plan of creation and redemption. He tells us how Father, Son, and Holy Spirit desire to dwell within us in the most intimate fashion, how they wish to share with us their own life through grace. All this he has accomplished and does accomplish through Christ. St. Paul tells us: "I became a minister of this Church through the commission God gave me to preach among you his word in its fullness, that mystery hidden from ages and generations past but now revealed to his holy ones. God has willed to make known to them the glory beyond price which this mystery brings to the Gentiles — the mystery of Christ in you, your hope of glory. This is the Christ we proclaim while we admonish all men and teach them in the full measure of wisdom, hoping to make every man complete in Christ" (Col 1:25-28)."

Excerpts from *Guiding Light – Feed My Soul*

p. 111 When Jesus said the two greatest commandments were about love: love of God and love of neighbor, the Jewish scholar asked Jesus another question: "And who is my neighbor?" You might recall that there was great animosity between Jews and Samaritans, so in introducing a Samaritan into the story, Jesus shows us "neighbor" could be anyone, even someone we despise.

p. 51 The conversation Jesus had about tragic events at the beginning of today's gospel was interesting. Sometimes people think when something bad happens to someone it is God's punishment. Jesus said that's not always true. He does not try to explain suffering here, but he is telling us not to be complacent, which we sometimes are. We can't think "well, if nothing bad is happening to me, it must be because I am so good." He tells us we all need to repent, i.e., to work to be better than we are.

pp. 29-30 As we celebrate Jesus' baptism, may we at the same time celebrate our own. May we rejoice in God's gift of love and life given to us, and may we live up to the high dignity with which God has blessed us.

A Priest Is a Gift from God

by Rita Ring

REFRAIN

C   F   C   Am   C

A priest is a gift from God. A priest is a gift from God.

F   C   F   G

This is My Bod - y, This is My Blood, A

VERSES 1, 3

C   F   C   C   F   G

priest is a gift from God. 1. Come to Me, My chil - dren,
3. Come to Me, chil-dren of God,

C   F   G   C   F   G

I want to pos-sess your soul, I love you so ten - der - ly,
I want to pos-sess your soul, I give My-self to___ you

C   F   G   C   F   C

I want you to love Me too, A priest is a gift from God.
in the Ho - ly Eu -cha-rist, A priest is a gift from God.

F   G   C   F   C

I tell you My chil - dren, a priest is a gift from God. To -
I tell you My chil - dren, a priest is a gift from God. To -

F   G   C   F   G

day is the day the Lord has made, Wake, My chil-dren from your sleep,
day is the day the Lord has made, Wake, My chil-dren from your sleep,

A Song from Jesus

by Rita Ring

I Love You Jesus

by Rita Ring

VERSES

C   F   G

1. Oh Burn-ing Heart, Oh Love di - vine, how
2. I can-not say. There are not words to
3. Your ten - der Heart, Oh how it beats for

C   F   G   C   F

sweet You are to me. I see the host, I
say what my heart feels. I love You so, I
love of each this day. I want to give You

G   Am   F   G   C

know You're here to love and care for me.
scarce can breathe when You come in - to me.
all my love, sur - ren - der to - tal - ly.

REFRAIN

C   F   G

I know Your love a lit - tle now, so

C   F   G   C   F

dear You are to me. Come give me life, a -

G   Am   F   G   C

bun - dant life, I thirst to be with Thee.

The Rosary Song

by Rita Rin

REFRAIN

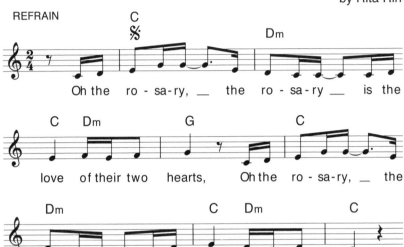

Oh the ro - sa-ry, __ the ro - sa-ry __ is the
love of their two hearts, Oh the ro - sa-ry, __ the
ro - sa-ry __ is the love of their two hearts.

VERSES 1-4

1. A - ve Ma - ri - a, A - ve Ma - ri - a. Oh the
2. Je - sus we love You, Ma - ry we love __ you. Oh the
3. This is her peace plan, Chil-dren must pray __ it. Oh the
4. We turn to Ma - ry, She is the Queen of Peace. Oh the

VERSE 5

No left hand

5. Oh Sa-cred Heart di - vine, Oh heart of Ma-ry pure,

A - ve Ma - ri - a, We love to pray it! Oh the

"This is My Body, This is My Blood."

Prayer Before the
Holy Sacrifice of the Mass

Let me be a holy sacrifice and unite with God in the sacrament of His greatest love.

I want to be one in Him in this act of love, where He gives Himself to me and I give myself as a sacrifice to Him. Let me be a holy sacrifice as I become one with Him in this my act of greatest love to Him.

Let me unite with Him more, that I may more deeply love Him. May I help make reparation to His adorable Heart and the heart of His Mother, Mary. With greatest love, I offer myself to You and pray that You will accept my sacrifice of greatest love. I give myself to You and unite in Your gift of Yourself to me. Come and possess my soul.

Cleanse me, strengthen me, heal me. Dear Holy Spirit act in the heart of Mary to make me more and more like Jesus.

Father, I offer this my sacrifice, myself united to Jesus in the Holy Spirit to You. Help me to love God more deeply in this act of my greatest love.

Give me the grace to grow in my knowledge, love and service of You and for this to be my greatest participation in the Mass. Give me the greatest graces to love You so deeply in this Mass, You who are so worthy of my love.

– *Mass Book*, December 27, 1995

Shepherds of Christ Associates

PRAYER MANUAL

Shepherds of Christ Publications
China, Indiana

Imprimi Potest: Rev. Bradley M. Schaeffer, S.J.
Provincial
Chicago Province, The Society of Jesus

Imprimatur: Most Rev. Carl K. Moeddel
Auxiliary Bishop
Archdiocese of Cincinnati

The Shepherds of Christ Associates Prayer Manual is published by
Shepherds of Christ Publications, an arm of Shepherds of Christ Ministries,
P.O. Box 627 Madison (China), Indiana 47250 USA.

Founder, Shepherds of Christ Ministries:
Father Edward J. Carter, S.J.

For more information contact:
Shepherds of Christ Associates
P.O. Box 627
Madison (China), Indiana 47250- USA
Tel. 812-273-8405
Toll Free: 1-888-211-3041
Fax 812-273-3182

First Printing, September 1994
Second Printing, November 1994
Third Printing, November 1995
Fourth Printing, March 1996

Chapter Meeting Prayer Format

The prayer format below should be followed at chapter meetings of *Shepherds of Christ Associates*. All prayers, not just those said specifically for priests, should include the intention of praying for all the needs of priests the world over.

1. **Hymns.** Hymns may be sung at any point of the prayer part of the meeting.

2. **Holy Spirit Prayer.** Come, Holy Spirit, almighty Sanctifier, God of love, who filled the Virgin Mary with grace, who wonderfully changed the hearts of the apostles, who endowed all Your martyrs with miraculous courage, come and sanctify us. Enlighten our minds, strengthen our wills, purify our consciences, rectify our judgment, set our hearts on fire, and preserve us from the misfortunes of resisting Your inspirations. Amen.

3. **The Rosary.**

4. **Salve Regina.** "Hail Holy Queen, Mother of mercy, our life, our sweetness, and our hope. To you do we cry, poor banished children of Eve. To you do we send up our sighs, our mourning, our weeping in this vale of tears. Turn, then, most gracious advocate, your eyes of mercy toward us and after this, our exile, show unto us the blessed fruit of your womb, Jesus, O clement, O loving, O sweet Virgin Mary. Amen."

5. **The Memorare.** "Remember, O most gracious Virgin Mary, that never was it known that anyone who fled to your protection, implored your help, or sought your intercession was left unaided. Inspired by this confidence, I fly unto you, O Virgin of virgins, my

Mother. To you I come, before you I stand, sinful and sorrowful. O Mother of the Word Incarnate, despise not my petitions, but, in your mercy, hear and answer me. Amen."

6. **Seven Hail Marys in honor of the Seven Sorrows of Mary.** Mary has promised very special graces to those who do this on a daily basis. Included in the promises of Our Lady for those who practice this devotion is her pledge to give special assistance at the hour of death, including the sight of her face. The seven sorrows are:

(1) The first sorrow: the prophecy of Simeon (Hail Mary).

(2) The second sorrow: the flight into Egypt (Hail Mary).

(3) The third sorrow: the loss of the Child Jesus in the temple (Hail Mary).

(4) The fourth sorrow: Jesus and Mary meet on the way to the cross (Hail Mary).

(5) The fifth sorrow: Jesus dies on the cross (Hail Mary).

(6) The sixth sorrow: Jesus is taken down from the cross and laid in Mary's arms (Hail Mary).

(7) The seventh sorrow: the burial of Jesus (Hail Mary).

7. **Litany of the Blessed Virgin Mary.**
   Lord, have mercy on us.
      Christ, have mercy on us.
   Lord, have mercy on us. Christ, hear us.
      Christ, graciously hear us.
   God, the Father of heaven, *have mercy on us.*
   God, the Son, Redeemer of the world,
      have mercy on us.
   God, the Holy Spirit, *have mercy on us.*

Holy Trinity, one God, *have mercy on us*.
Holy Mary, *pray for us* (repeat after each invocation).
Holy Mother of God,
Holy Virgin of virgins,
Mother of Christ,
Mother of the Church,
Mother of divine grace,
Mother most pure,
Mother most chaste,
Mother inviolate,
Mother undefiled,
Mother most amiable,
Mother most admirable,
Mother of good counsel,
Mother of our Creator,
Mother of our Savior,
Virgin most prudent,
Virgin most venerable,
Virgin most renowned,
Virgin most powerful,
Virgin most merciful,
Virgin most faithful,
Mirror of justice,
Seat of wisdom,
Cause of our joy,
Spiritual vessel,
Vessel of honor,
Singular vessel of devotion,
Mystical rose,
Tower of David,
Tower of ivory,
House of gold,
Ark of the Covenant,
Gate of heaven,

Morning star,
Health of the sick,
Refuge of sinners,
Comforter of the afflicted,
Help of Christians,
Queen of angels,
Queen of patriarchs,
Queen of prophets,
Queen of apostles,
Queen of martyrs,
Queen of confessors,
Queen of virgins,
Queen of all saints,
Queen conceived without original sin,
Queen assumed into heaven,
Queen of the most holy rosary,
Queen of families,
Queen of peace,
Lamb of God, who take away the sins of the world,
  spare us, O Lord.
Lamb of God, who take away the sins of the world,
  graciously hear us, O Lord.
Lamb of God, who take away the sins of the world,
  have mercy on us.
Pray for us, O holy Mother of God,
  that we may be made worthy of the promises of Christ.

Let us pray: Grant, we beseech You, O Lord God, that we Your servants may enjoy perpetual health of mind and body and, by the glorious intercession of the blessed Mary, ever virgin, be delivered from present sorrow, and obtain eternal joy. Through Christ our Lord. Amen.

We fly to your patronage, O holy Mother of God. Despise not our petitions in our necessities, but deliver us always from all dangers, O glorious and blessed Virgin. Amen.

8. **Prayer to St. Joseph.** St. Joseph, guardian of Jesus and chaste spouse of Mary, you passed your life in perfect fulfillment of duty. You supported the Holy Family of Nazareth with the work of your hands. Kindly protect those who trustingly turn to you. You know their aspirations, their hardships, their hopes; and they turn to you because they know you will understand and protect them. You too have known trial, labor, and weariness. But, even amid the worries of material life, your soul was filled with deep peace and sang out in true joy through intimacy with the Son of God entrusted to you, and with Mary, His tender Mother. Amen.

— *(Pope John XXIII)*

9. **Litany of the Sacred Heart, promises of the Sacred Heart.**
Lord, have mercy on us.
   Christ, have mercy on us.
Lord, have mercy on us. Christ, hear us.
   Christ, graciously hear us.
God the Father of heaven,
   have mercy on us (repeat after each invocation).
God the Son, Redeemer of the world,
God the Holy Spirit,
Holy Trinity, one God,
Heart of Jesus, Son of the eternal Father,
Heart of Jesus, formed by the Holy Spirit in the womb of the Virgin Mother,
Heart of Jesus, substantially united to the Word of God,
Heart of Jesus, of infinite majesty,

Heart of Jesus, sacred temple of God,
Heart of Jesus, tabernacle of the Most High,
Heart of Jesus, house of God and gate of heaven,
Heart of Jesus, burning furnace of charity,
Heart of Jesus, abode of justice and love,
Heart of Jesus, full of goodness and love,
Heart of Jesus, abyss of all virtues,
Heart of Jesus, most worthy of all praise,
Heart of Jesus, king and center of all hearts,
Heart of Jesus, in whom are all the treasures of
  wisdom and knowledge,
Heart of Jesus, in whom dwells the fullness of
  divinity,
Heart of Jesus, in whom the Father is well pleased,
Heart of Jesus, of whose fullness we have all
  received,
Heart of Jesus, desire of the everlasting hills,
Heart of Jesus, patient and most merciful,
Heart of Jesus, enriching all who invoke You,
Heart of Jesus, fountain of life and holiness,
Heart of Jesus, propitiation for our sins,
Heart of Jesus, loaded down with opprobrium,
Heart of Jesus, bruised for our offenses,
Heart of Jesus, obedient even to death,
Heart of Jesus, pierced with a lance,
Heart of Jesus, source of all consolation,
Heart of Jesus, our life and reconciliation,
Heart of Jesus, victim of sin,
Heart of Jesus, salvation of those who hope in You,
Heart of Jesus, hope of those who die in You,
Heart of Jesus, delight of all the saints,
Lamb of God, Who take away the sins of the world,
  spare us, O Lord.
Lamb of God, Who take away the sins of the world,

graciously hear us, O Lord.
Lamb of God, Who take away the sins of the world,
   have mercy on us.
Jesus, meek and humble of heart,
   make our hearts like unto Yours.

Let us pray: O almighty and eternal God, look upon the Heart of Your dearly beloved Son and upon the praise and satisfaction He offers You in behalf of sinners and, being appeased, grant pardon to those who seek Your mercy, in the name of the same Jesus Christ, Your Son, Who lives and reigns with You, in the unity of the Holy Spirit, world without end. Amen.

Promises of Our Lord to those devoted to His Sacred Heart (these should be read by the prayer leader):

(1) I will give them all the graces necessary in their state of life.
(2) I will establish peace in their homes.
(3) I will comfort them in all their afflictions.
(4) I will be their refuge during life and above all in death.
(5) I will bestow a large blessing on all their undertakings.
(6) Sinners shall find in My Heart the source and the infinite ocean of mercy.
(7) Tepid souls shall grow fervent.
(8) Fervent souls shall quickly mount to high perfection.
(9) I will bless every place where a picture of My Heart shall be set up and honored.
(10) I will give to priests the gift of touching the most hardened hearts.
(11) Those who promote this devotion shall have their names written in My Heart, never to be blotted out.

(12) I promise you in the excessive mercy of My Heart that My all-powerful love will grant to all those who communicate on the first Friday in nine consecutive months the grace of final penitence; they shall not die in My disgrace nor without receiving their sacraments; My divine Heart shall be their safe refuge in this last moment.

10. **Prayer for Priests.** "Lord Jesus, Chief Shepherd of the Flock, we pray that in the great love and mercy of Your Sacred Heart You attend to all the needs of Your priest-shepherds throughout the world. We ask that You draw back to Your Heart all those priests who have seriously strayed from Your path, that You rekindle the desire for holiness in the hearts of those priests who have become lukewarm, and that You continue to give Your fervent priests the desire for the highest holiness. United with Your Heart and Mary's Heart, we ask that You take this petition to Your heavenly Father in the unity of the Holy Spirit. Amen."

11. **Prayer for all members of the Shepherds of Christ Associates.** "Dear Jesus, we ask Your special blessings on all members of Shepherds of Christ Associates. Continue to enlighten them regarding the very special privilege and responsibility you have given them as members of Your movement, Shepherds of Christ Associates. Draw them ever closer to Your Heart and to Your Mother's Heart. Allow them to more and more realize the great and special love of Your Hearts for each of them as unique individuals. Give them the grace to respond to Your love and Mary's love with an increased love of their own. As they dwell in Your Heart and Mary's Heart, abundantly care for all their needs and those of their loved ones. We make our

prayer through You to the Father, in the Holy Spirit, with Mary our Mother at our side. Amen."

12. **Prayer for the spiritual and financial success of the priestly newsletter.** "Father, we ask Your special blessings upon the priestly newsletter, Shepherds of Christ. We ask that You open the priest-readers to the graces You wish to give them through this chosen instrument of Your Son. We also ask that You provide for the financial needs of the newsletter and the Shepherds of Christ Associates. We make our prayer through Jesus, in the Holy Spirit, with Mary at our side. Amen."

13. **Prayer for all members of the human family.** "Heavenly Father, we ask Your blessings on all Your children the world over. Attend to all their needs. We ask Your special assistance for all those marginalized people, all those who are so neglected and forgotten. United with our Mother Mary, we make this petition to You through Jesus and in the Holy Spirit. Amen."

14. **Prayer to St. Michael and our Guardian Angels:** "St. Michael the Archangel, defend us in battle. Be our safeguard against the wickedness and snares of the devil. May God rebuke him, we humbly pray, and do thou, O prince of the heavenly hosts, by the power of God, cast into hell Satan and all the other evil spirits who prowl about the world seeking the ruin of souls. Amen."
"Angel of God, my guardian dear, to whom God's love commits me here, ever this day be at my side, to light and guard, to rule and guide. Amen."

15. **Pause for silent, personal prayer.** This should last at least five minutes.

16. **Act of consecration to the Sacred Heart of Jesus and the Immaculate Heart of Mary.**

"Lord Jesus, Chief Shepherd of the flock, I consecrate myself to Your most Sacred Heart. From Your pierced Heart the Church was born, the Church You have called me, as a member of Shepherds of Christ Associates, to serve in a most special way. You reveal Your Heart as a symbol of Your love in all its aspects, including Your most special love for me, whom You have chosen as Your companion in this most important work. Help me to always love You in return. Help me to give myself entirely to You. Help me always to pour out my life in love of God and neighbor! Heart of Jesus, I place my trust in You!

"Dear Blessed Virgin Mary, I consecrate myself to your maternal and Immaculate Heart, this Heart which is symbol of your life of love. You are the Mother of my Savior. You are also my Mother. You love me with a most special love as a member of Shepherds of Christ Associates, a movement created by your Son as a powerful instrument for the renewal of the Church and the world. In a return of love, I give myself entirely to your motherly love and protection. You followed Jesus perfectly. You are His first and perfect disciple. Teach me to imitate you in the putting on of Christ. Be my motherly intercessor so that, through your Immaculate Heart, I may be guided to an ever closer union with the pierced Heart of Jesus, Chief Shepherd of the flock."

17. **Daily Prayers.** All members should say the Holy Spirit prayer daily and make the act of consecration daily. They should also pray the rosary each day. They are encouraged to use the other above prayers as time allows.

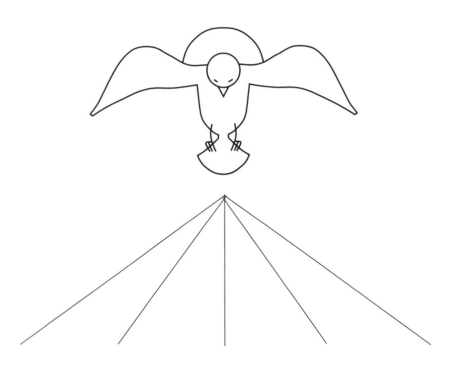

HOLY SPIRIT NOVENA

**The Holy Spirit Novnea prayers are
also available in
Spanish, French, and Portuguese.**

Shepherds of Christ Publications
China, Indiana

This book is published by Shepherds of Christ Publications, a subsidiary of Shepherds of Christ Ministries, a tax exempt religious public charitable association organized to foster devotion to the Two Hearts, the Sacred Heart of Jesus and the Immaculate Heart of Mary.

For additional copies, contact us:

Shepherds of Christ Ministries
  P.O. Box 627
  Madison (China), Indiana 47250 USA

(toll free number) 1-888-211-3041

(phone) 1-812-273-8405

(fax) 1-812-273-3182

http://www.SofC.org

Nihil Obstat:
  Rev. Daniel J. Mahan, S.T.L.
  Censor Librorum
  Archdiocese of Indianapolis

Imprimatur:
  Archbishop Daniel M. Buechlein, O.S.B.
  Archbishop of Indianapolis
  Archdiocese of Indianapolis

First Printing: March, 1999
Second Printing: April, 2000

DAILY NOVENA PRAYERS

Opening Prayer

In the name of the Father and of the Son and of the Holy Spirit. Amen.

Dear Father, we come to You in the name of Jesus, in union with Him in the Holy Sacrifice of the Mass, in the Holy Spirit. We come to You united to the Child Jesus of Good Health and the Infant of Prague. We come to You in the perfect, sinless heart of Our Mother Mary, asking her powerful intercession, uniting ourselves to her holy tears. We come to You united to all the angels and saints, and the souls in purgatory.

Prayer for Holy Spirit

We pray for an outpouring of the Holy Spirit on us, to be baptized by the Holy Spirit, that He will descend mightily on us as He did on the Apostles at Pentecost. That the Holy Spirit will transform us from fear to fearlessness and that He will give us courage to do all the Father is asking of us to help bring about the Reign of the Sacred Heart and the triumph of Mary's Immaculate Heart. We pray for the Holy Spirit to descend mightily on the Jesuits and the Poor Clares on the Shepherds of Christ leaders and members and on the whole Body of Christ and the world.

Protection by the Blood of Jesus

We pray that the Blood of Jesus will be spread on us, everyone in our families, and the Shepherds of Christ Movement, that we will be able to move steadfastly ahead and be protected from the evil one.

Healing

We pray for healing in body, mind, and soul and generational healing in ourselves, in all members in our families, and in all members of the Shepherds of Christ Movement, the Jesuit Community, the Poor Clares, the Body of Christ, and the world.

Prayer for Strength and Light

We adore You, oh Holy Spirit. Give us strength, give us light, console us. We give ourselves entirely to You. Oh Spirit of light and grace, we want to only do the will of the Father. Enlighten us that we may live always in the Father's will.

Eternal Spirit fill us with Your Divine Wisdom that we may comprehend more fully insight into Your Divine Mysteries.

Give us lights, Oh Holy Spirit that we may know God. Work within the heart, the spiritual womb of the Virgin Mary, to form us more and more into the image of Jesus.

Prayer to Be One with God, Father, Son and Holy Spirit

We long for You, Oh Spirit of Light, we long to know God, we want to be one with Him, our Divine God. We want to be one with the Father, know Him as a Person most intimately. We want to know the beloved One, the Sacred Heart of Jesus, and live and dwell in Him at all times, every moment of our lives. We want to be one with You, Oh Spirit of Light, that You move in us in our every breath.

Prayer to Be One in Jesus

Let us experience life in the Sacred Heart of Jesus, so we can say as Saint Paul, "I have been crucified with Christ and yet I am alive; yet it is no longer I, but Christ living in me...." Let us live, united to the Mass, all through the day being one in Him. Let us be able to love and know in this elevated state of oneness with our God. We long for Thee, oh beauteous God, we love You, we love You, we love You. We praise You, worship You, honor You, adore You, and thank You, our beloved God, Father, Son, and Holy Spirit.

Prayer to Dwell in the Hearts of Jesus and Mary

We seek to be one in God, to live and dwell in the Hearts of Jesus and Mary, our little heaven on earth, to experience life in the all perfect, pure, sinless heart of our Mother. We want the Holy Spirit to move in us and to be united to Jesus as the Bridegroom of our souls and be a most perfect sacrifice offered to the Father at every moment as we unite in the Holy Sacrifice of the Mass around the world to help in the salvation of souls.

Prayer for the Holy Spirit and His Gifts

Come Holy Spirit, come, come into our hearts, inflame all people with the fire of Your love.

Leader: Send forth Your Spirit and all will be reborn.

All: And You will renew the face of the earth.

We pray for the seven gifts of the Holy Spirit, we ask for perfection in our souls to make us holy, holy souls likened to God.

Dear Holy Spirit, we give ourselves to You soul and body. We ask You to give us the Spirit of Wisdom, Understanding, Counsel, Fortitude, Knowledge, Piety, and Fear of the Lord.

Prayer for the Word Alive in Our Hearts

We know, dear Holy Spirit, the Word in His human nature was brought forth within the womb of the woman. We pray that His word will be brought forth in our hearts as He lives and dwells in us. We want the incarnation to go on in our lives. Dear Holy Spirit, work in us.

Little Prayers to the Holy Spirit

Dear Holy Spirit, help us not to be ignorant or indifferent or weak, help us to be strong with the love of God.

Dear Holy Spirit, please pray for our needs for us.

Dear Holy Spirit, help us to respect God and to avoid sin. Help us to live in the Father's will.

Dear Holy Spirit, help us to keep Your commandments and to respect authority. Help us to love all things as You will us to love them. Help us to want to pray and always serve God with the greatest love. Help us to know the truth. Help us to have the gift of faith, hope, and love. Help us to know what is right and what is wrong.

A Prayer for Intimacy with the Lamb, the Bridegroom of the Soul

Oh Lamb of God, Who take away the sins of the world, come and act on my soul most intimately. I surrender myself, as I ask for the grace to let go, to just be as I exist in You and You act most intimately on my soul. You are the Initiator. I am the soul waiting Your favors as You act in me. I love You. I adore You. I worship You. Come and possess my soul with Your Divine Grace, as I experience You most intimately.

FIRST WEEK
MEDITATIONS NINE DAYS

1. Romans 8:14-17
All who are guided by the Spirit of God are sons of God; for what you received was not the spirit of slavery to bring you back into fear; you received the Spirit of adoption, enabling us to cry out, 'Abba, Father!' The Spirit himself joins with our spirit to bear witness that we are children of God. And if we are children, then we are heirs, heirs of God and joint-heirs with Christ, provided that we share his suffering, so as to share his glory.

2. Romans 8:5-9
Those who are living by their natural inclinations have their minds on the things human nature desires; those who live in the Spirit have their minds on spiritual things. And human nature has nothing to look forward to but death, while the Spirit looks forward to life and peace, because the outlook of disordered human nature is opposed to God, since it does not submit to God's Law, and indeed it cannot, and those who live by their natural inclinations can never be pleasing to God. You, however, live not by your natural inclinations, but by the Spirit, since the Spirit of God has made a home in you. Indeed, anyone who does not have the Spirit of Christ does not belong to him.

3. 1 John 4:12-16
No one has ever seen God, but as long as we love one another God remains in us and his love comes to its perfection in us. This is the proof that we remain in him and he in us, that he has given us a share in his Spirit. We ourselves have seen and testify that the Father sent his Son as Saviour of the world. Anyone who acknowledges that Jesus is the Son of God, God remains in him and he in God. We have recognised for

ourselves, and put our faith in, the love God has for us.
God is love, and whoever remains in love remains in
God and God in him.

4. 1 John 4:17-21
Love comes to its perfection in us when we can face
the Day of Judgement fearlessly, because even in this
world we have become as he is. In love there is no room
for fear, but perfect love drives out fear, because fear
implies punishment and no one who is afraid has come
to perfection in love. Let us love, then, because he first
loved us. Anyone who says 'I love God' and hates his
brother, is a liar, since whoever does not love the
brother whom he can see cannot love God whom he
has not seen. Indeed this is the commandment we have
received from him, that whoever loves God, must also
love his brother.

5. 1 John 4:7-11
My dear friends, let us love one another, since love
is from God and everyone who loves is a child of God
and knows God. Whoever fails to love does not know
God, because God is love. This is the revelation of
God's love for us, that God sent his only Son into the
world that we might have life through him. Love
consists in this: it is not we who loved God, but God
loved us and sent his Son to expiate our sins. My dear
friends, if God loved us so much, we too should love
one another.

6. Acts of the Apostles 1:1-5
In my earlier work, Theophilus, I dealt with
everything Jesus had done and taught from the
beginning until the day he gave his instructions to the
apostles he had chosen through the Holy Spirit, and
was taken up to heaven. He had shown himself alive
to them after his Passion by many demonstrations:
for forty days he had continued to appear to them and
tell them about the kingdom of God. While at table
with them, he had told them not to leave Jerusalem,

but to wait there for what the Father had promised. 'It is', he had said, 'what you have heard me speak about: John baptised with water but, not many days from now, you are going to be baptised with the Holy Spirit.'

7.   Acts of the Apostles 1:6-9

Now having met together, they asked him, 'Lord, has the time come for you to restore the kingdom to Israel?' He replied, 'It is not for you to know times or dates that the Father has decided by his own authority, but you will receive the power of the Holy Spirit which will come on you, and then you will be my witnesses not only in Jerusalem but throughout Judaea and Samaria, and indeed to earth's remotest end.'

As he said this he was lifted up while they looked on, and a cloud took him from their sight.

8.   Acts of the Apostles 1:12-14

So from the Mount of Olives, as it is called, they went back to Jerusalem, a short distance away, no more than a Sabbath walk; and when they reached the city they went to the upper room where they were staying; there were Peter and John, James and Andrew, Philip and Thomas, Bartholomew and Matthew, James son of Alphaeus and Simon the Zealot, and Jude son of James. With one heart all these joined constantly in prayer, together with some women, including Mary the mother of Jesus, and with his brothers.

9.   Acts of the Apostles 2:1-4

When Pentecost day came round, they had all met together, when suddenly there came from heaven a sound as of a violent wind which filled the entire house in which they were sitting; and there appeared to them tongues as of fire; these separated and came to rest on the head of each of them. They were all filled with the Holy Spirit and began to speak different languages as the Spirit gave them power to express themselves.

SECOND WEEK
MEDITATIONS NINE DAYS

1. **John 14:21-31**
Whoever holds to my commandments and keeps them is the one who loves me; and whoever loves me will be loved by my Father, and I shall love him and reveal myself to him.'

Judas—not Judas Iscariot—said to him, 'Lord, what has happened, that you intend to show yourself to us and not to the world?' Jesus replied:

'Anyone who loves me will keep my word, and my Father will love him, and we shall come to him and make a home in him. Anyone who does not love me does not keep my words. And the word that you hear is not my own: it is the word of the Father who sent me. I have said these things to you while still with you; but the Paraclete, the Holy Spirit, whom the Father will send in my name, will teach you everything and remind you of all I have said to you. Peace I bequeath to you, my own peace I give you, a peace which the world cannot give, this is my gift to you. Do not let your hearts be troubled or afraid. You heard me say: I am going away and shall return. If you loved me you would be glad that I am going to the Father, for the Father is greater than I. I have told you this now, before it happens, so that when it does happen you may believe.

'I shall not talk to you much longer, because the prince of this world is on his way. He has no power over me, but the world must recognise that I love the Father and that I act just as the Father commanded. Come now, let us go.

2. **John 17:11-26**
I am no longer in the world, but they are in the world, and I am coming to you. Holy Father, keep those you have given me true to your name, so that

they may be one like us. While I was with them, I kept those you had given me true to your name. I have watched over them and not one is lost except one who was destined to be lost, and this was to fulfil the scriptures. But now I am coming to you and I say these things in the world to share my joy with them to the full. I passed your word on to them, and the world hated them, because they belong to the world no more than I belong to the world. I am not asking you to remove them from the world, but to protect them from the Evil One. They do not belong to the world any more than I belong to the world. Consecrate them in the truth; your word is truth. As you sent me into the world, I have sent them into the world, and for their sake I consecrate myself so that they too may be consecrated in truth. I pray not only for these but also for those who through their teaching will come to believe in me. May they all be one, just as, Father, you are in me and I am in you, so that they also may be in us, so that the world may believe it was you who sent me. I have given them the glory you gave to me, that they may be one as we are one. With me in them and you in me, may they be so perfected in unity that the world will recognise that it was you who sent me and that you have loved them as you have loved me.

Father, I want those you have given me to be with me where I am, so that they may always see my glory which you have given me because you loved me before the foundation of the world. Father, Upright One, the world has not known you, but I have known you, and these have known that you have sent me. I have made your name known to them and will continue to make it known, so that the love with which you loved me may be in them, and so that I may be in them.

3. 1 Corinthians 15:20-28

In fact, however, Christ has been raised from the dead, as the first-fruits of all who have fallen asleep. As it was by one man that death came, so through one man has come the resurrection of the dead. Just as all die in Adam, so in Christ all will be brought to life; but all of them in their proper order: Christ the first-fruits, and next, at his coming, those who belong to him. After that will come the end, when he will hand over the kingdom to God the Father, having abolished every principality, every ruling force and power. For he is to be king until he has made his enemies his footstool, and the last of the enemies to be done away with is death, for he has put all things under his feet. But when it is said everything is subjected, this obviously cannot include the One who subjected everything to him. When everything has been subjected to him, then the Son himself will be subjected to the One who has subjected everything to him, so that God may be all in all.

4. Revelation 3:1-3,12,16-19

'Write to the angel of the church in Sardis and say, "Here is the message of the one who holds the seven spirits of God and the seven stars: I know about your behaviour: how you are reputed to be alive and yet are dead. Wake up; put some resolve into what little vigour you have left: it is dying fast. So far I have failed to notice anything in your behaviour that my God could possibly call perfect; remember how you first heard the message. Hold on to that. Repent! If you do not wake up, I shall come to you like a thief, and you will have no idea at what hour I shall come upon you.

Anyone who proves victorious I will make into a pillar in the sanctuary of my God, and it will stay there for ever; I will inscribe on it the name of my God and the name of the city of my God, the new Jerusalem which is coming down from my God in heaven, and my own new name as well.

'...but since you are neither hot nor cold, but only lukewarm, I will spit you out of my mouth. You say to yourself: I am rich, I have made a fortune and have everything I want, never realising that you are wretchedly and pitiably poor, and blind and naked too. I warn you, buy from me the gold that has been tested in the fire to make you truly rich, and white robes to clothe you and hide your shameful nakedness, and ointment to put on your eyes to enable you to see. I reprove and train those whom I love: so repent in real earnest.'

5. Revelation 5:9-14

They sang a new hymn: You are worthy to take the scroll and to break its seals, because you were sacrificed, and with your blood you bought people for God of every race, language, people and nation and made them a line of kings and priests for God, to rule the world.

In my vision, I heard the sound of an immense number of angels gathered round the throne and the living creatures and the elders; there were ten thousand times ten thousand of them and thousands upon thousands, loudly chanting:

Worthy is the Lamb that was sacrificed to receive power, riches, wisdom, strength, honour, glory and blessing. Then I heard all the living things in creation—everything that lives in heaven, and on earth, and under the earth, and in the sea, crying:

To the One seated on the throne and to the Lamb, be all praise, honour, glory and power, for ever and ever.

And the four living creatures said, 'Amen'; and the elders prostrated themselves to worship.

6. Revelation 7:14-17

I answered him, 'You can tell me, sir.' Then he said, 'These are the people who have been through the great trial; they have washed their robes white again in the blood of the Lamb. That is why they are standing in front of God's throne and serving him day and night in his sanctuary; and the One who sits on the throne will spread his tent over them. They will never hunger or thirst again; sun and scorching wind will never plague them, because the Lamb who is at the heart of the throne will be their shepherd and will guide them to springs of living water; and God will wipe away all tears from their eyes.'

7. Revelation 12:1-8

Now a great sign appeared in heaven: a woman, robed with the sun, standing on the moon, and on her head a crown of twelve stars. She was pregnant, and in labour, crying aloud in the pangs of childbirth. Then a second sign appeared in the sky: there was a huge red dragon with seven heads and ten horns, and each of the seven heads crowned with a coronet. Its tail swept a third of the stars from the sky and hurled them to the ground, and the dragon stopped in front of the woman as she was at the point of giving birth, so that it could eat the child as soon as it was born. The woman was delivered of a boy, the son who was to rule all the nations with an iron sceptre, and the child was taken straight up to God and to his throne, while the woman escaped into the desert, where God had prepared a place for her to be looked after for twelve hundred and sixty days.

And now war broke out in heaven, when Michael with his angels attacked the dragon. The dragon fought back with his angels, but they were defeated and driven out of heaven.

8. Revelation 14:1-7

Next in my vision I saw Mount Zion, and standing on it the Lamb who had with him a hundred and forty-four thousand people, all with his name and his Father's name written on their foreheads. I heard a sound coming out of heaven like the sound of the ocean or the roar of thunder; it was like the sound of harpists playing their harps. There before the throne they were singing a new hymn in the presence of the four living creatures and the elders, a hymn that could be learnt only by the hundred and forty-four thousand who had been redeemed from the world. These are the sons who have kept their virginity and not been defiled with women; they follow the Lamb wherever he goes; they, out of all people, have been redeemed to be the first-fruits for God and for the Lamb. No lie was found in their mouths and no fault can be found in them.

Then I saw another angel, flying high overhead, sent to announce the gospel of eternity to all who live on the earth, every nation, race, language and tribe. He was calling, 'Fear God and glorify him, because the time has come for him to sit in judgement; worship the maker of heaven and earth and sea and the springs of water.'

Revelation 19: 7-8

let us be glad and joyful and give glory to God, because this is the time for the marriage of the Lamb. His bride is ready, and she has been able to dress herself in dazzling white linen, because her linen is made of the good deeds of the saints.'

9.   Revelation 21:1-10

Then I saw a new heaven and a new earth; the first heaven and the first earth had disappeared now, and there was no longer any sea. I saw the holy city, the new Jerusalem, coming down out of heaven from God, prepared as a bride dressed for her husband. Then I heard a loud voice call from the throne, 'Look, here God lives among human beings. He will make his home among them; they will be his people, and he will be their God, God-with-them. He will wipe away all tears from their eyes; there will be no more death, and no more mourning or sadness or pain. The world of the past has gone.'

Then the One sitting on the throne spoke. 'Look, I am making the whole of creation new. Write this, "What I am saying is trustworthy and will come true."' Then he said to me, 'It has already happened. I am the Alpha and the Omega, the Beginning and the End. I will give water from the well of life free to anybody who is thirsty; anyone who proves victorious will inherit these things; and I will be his God and he will be my son. But the legacy for cowards, for those who break their word, or worship obscenities, for murderers and the sexually immoral, and for sorcerers, worshippers of false gods or any other sort of liars, is the second death in the burning lake of sulphur.'

One of the seven angels that had the seven bowls full of the seven final plagues came to speak to me and said, 'Come here and I will show you the bride that the Lamb has married.' In the spirit, he carried me to the top of a very high mountain, and showed me Jerusalem, the holy city, coming down out of heaven from God.

Revelation 22:20

The one who attests these things says: I am indeed coming soon.

Amen; come, Lord Jesus.

Scriptural quotations are taken from
The New Jerusalem Bible, Doubleday & Co.
Imprimatur granted by Cardinal Hume.

Prayer for Union with Jesus

Come to me, Lord, and possess my soul. Come into my heart and permeate my soul. Help me to sit in silence with You and let You work in my heart.

I am Yours to possess. I am Yours to use. I want to be selfless and only exist in You. Help me to spoon out all that is me and be an empty vessel ready to be filled by You. Help me to die to myself and live only for You. Use me as You will. Let me never draw my attention back to myself. I only want to operate as You do, dwelling within me.

I am Yours, Lord. I want to have my life in You. I want to do the will of the Father. Give me the strength to put aside the world and let You operate my very being. Help me to act as You desire. Strengthen me against the distractions of the devil to take me from Your work.

When I worry, I have taken my focus off of You and placed it on myself. Help me not to give in to the promptings of others to change what in my heart You are making very clear to me. I worship You, I adore You and I love You. Come and dwell in me now.

150 Year Celebration of St Boniface as a Parish and Father Joe's 50th Celebration of Ordination

IN REMEMBRANCE
OF MY
FIFTIETH ANNIVERSARY
OF PRIESTLY ORDINATION

Rev. JOSEPH A. ROBINSON
1964   MAY   2014

Let us Pray for one another

Baptism

Eucharist

Confirmation

Confirmation

Marriage

Rita Robinson Ring and Fr. Joseph Robinson

Other great books published by Shepherds of Christ Publications
(To order call or write us at address in front of book)

Shepherds of Christ Prayer Manual
The Shepherds of Christ has prayer chapters all over the world praying for the priests, the Church and the world. These prayers that Father Carter compiled in the summer of 1994 began this worldwide network of prayer. Currently the prayers are in eight languages with the Church's *Imprimatur*. We have prayed daily for the priests, the Church, and the world since 1994. Associates are called to join prayer Chapters and help us circulate the newsletter centered on spreading devotion to the Sacred Heart and Immaculate Heart and helping to renew the Church through greater holiness. Please form a Prayer Chapter & order a Prayer Manual. Item P1 - $0.50

Spirituality Handbook Fr. Edward Carter, S.J. did 3 synopsis of the spiritual life. *The Spirituality Handbook, the Priestly Newsletter 2000 Issue 3* and the *Tell My People* book. The way of spiritual life proposed to the members of Shepherds of Christ Associates is centered in consecration to the Hearts of Jesus and Mary. All aspects of the spiritual life discussed below should be viewed as means to help members develop their lives in consecration to Christ, the Sacred Heart, and to Mary, the Immaculate Heart. Item P2 - $3

Fr. Edward J. Carter S.J.

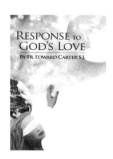

Response to God's Love by Fr. Edward J. Carter, S.J. In this book Fr. Carter speaks of God as the ultimate mystery. We can meditate on the interior life of the Trinity. Fr. Carter tells us about our uniqueness in the Father's Plan for us, how the individual Christian, the Church and the world are in the state of becoming. *Imprimatur*. Item BN4 -$10

Response in Christ by Fr. Carter - The book, *Response in Christ*, comes at a very opportune time. In a thoughtful blend of the traditional and the modern, Fr. Carter gives to the modern Christian a message that will sustain him. The most promising aspect of the book is Fr. Carter's gift about the Spiritual life. The Christian life essentially consists in God's loving self-communication to us with our response to Him in love. God gives us a sharing in His life in baptism. This life is nourished by the Eucharist. Father Carter offers reflections on how to deepen one's relationship with God: Father, Son and Holy Spirit. Item BN5 -$10

Shepherds of Christ - Selected Writings on Spirituality for all People as Published in Shepherds of Christ Newsletter for Priests. Contains 12 issues of the newsletter from July/August 1994 to May/June 1996. Item BN1 - $15

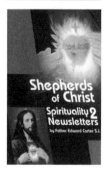

Shepherds of Christ - Volume 2 by Fr. Edward J. Carter, S.J. Contains issues 13-29 of the Priestly newsletter (September/ October 1996 - Issue 5, 1999) Item BN2 - $15

Fr. Edward J. Carter S.J.

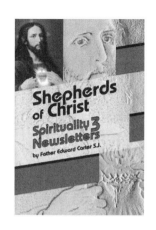

Shepherds of Christ - Volume 3 by Fr. Edward J. Carter, S.J. Contains Priestly Newsletter Issues 1 through 4 of 2000 including Fr. Carter's tremendous *Overview of the Spiritual Life*
Item BN3 - $10

Rita Ring

Mass Book, by Rita Ring. Many of the entries in the Priestly Newsletter Volume II from a spiritual journal came from this book. These entries are to help people to be more deeply united to God in the Mass. This book is available in English and Spanish with the Church's *Imprimatur*.
Item B8 - $12

Parents and Children's Rosary Book, by Rita Ring. Short Meditations for both parents and children to be used when praying the rosary. These meditations will help all to know the lives of Jesus and Mary alive in their Hearts. Available in both English and Spanish with the Church's *Imprimatur*.
Item B7 - $10

Fr. Joe Robinson
(Rita Ring's Brother)

Guiding Light - Focusing on the Word - Cycle B — At times we may feel that our path to Christ is a bit "out of focus". Like the disciples in the Book of Mark, this ordinary life clouds our vision of Christ's Divinity. We may doubt the practicality or possibility of applying His teachings and example to our modern life. Cycle B's homilies are a "guiding light" to help us realize Jesus' Messianic greatness and His promise of better things to come. Item C2 - $15

Feed My Soul - Cycle C — In a world rapidly advancing and encouraging personal gain, we are faced with modern problems. There is a challenge to find time in our busy schedules for Sunday Mass or a family meal. We are able to research, shop, bank and even work without hearing one human voice. It is no wonder that we may often feel disconnected and famished at our week's end. In Fr. Joe's third book of homilies from Cycle C, we are reminded of the charity that Christ intended us to show each other. .... We are rewarded with the Father's kingdom and love when we are not worthy. We are not left alone or hungry. Item C3 - $15

Steadfast to the Son - Cycle A — The sunflower is a great example of how we should be steadfastly guided by light. What a powerful thought that this exceptional plant is not stuck in one pose day in and day out, yet adaptable and magnetized to the sun. We feel the same about our Son. Our heads turns to face Christ as each day presents its challenges to find light. We join together like plants in a field and soak up the Son through the pulpit. We are a warm circle of strength using the wind of our breath to carry our priests' words, Christ's words, to new rich soil. Item C4 - $15

Guiding Light - Reflect on the Word - Cycle B — The Word leaves an impression on our souls. In my thoughts and reflections are born a more tangible understanding of these eternal concepts presented in the Gospels and the readings. Anyone can read a sentence, but not anyone can absorb it's true meaning. Truth, in this day and age, is almost a matter of opinion or individual entitlement. We believe that Christ's truth is our Roman Catholic Church. We, as priests, champion it's teachings; we are ambassadors for the Pope and Christ to those faces looking at us. We are the light by which our congregation reads to reflect upon real truth and we do it hand in hand. Item C5 - $15

Guiding Light - Centered In Christ, Cycle C — In the gospel of St. Luke, Christ turns toward Jerusalem, making the choice of love through sacrifice. In the silence of our own hearts, we find a worthy call to action. What personal path will you chose as you center in Jesus Christ? Fr. Joseph Robinson has dedicated his life to serving Christ and the Church from the Cincinnati Archdiocese in Ohio for over 40 years. He inspires his parishioners with the homilies found in these pages. ... May they be a guiding light for you as they have been for so many others. Item C6 -$10

Guiding Light - Inspired To Be Genuine, Cycle A

We look over the pulpit, like a father over Sunday breakfast and we want to connect. We want our parishioners to know the fulfillment, wisdom and desire that inspired our vows. We want them to find Christ and each other in Christ. Like a father, we want their attention, love and respect.

Privately, their minds may be else-where: in the next meeting, compiling a grocery list, worrying about a child, or angry with their spouse. We all leave a proverbial tornado of obligatory noise at the church doors to enjoy a single hour of unhurried glory. ... Father Joe Robinson inspires this appreciation into focus with humor, interesting facts and fresh perspectives. His homilies are easily followed, yet "meaty". May we all succeed to enliven a tangible God in the heart's forefront of those who hear us. Item C7 - $10

By God Through Me, Cycle B - It can be challenging to remain alive to the magnitude of the role that I perform as a priest, a servant of God, a shepherd to the world, a sacramental sign of Christ... I wake up, eat, brush my teeth, get dressed and then transform bread into Flesh and wine into Blood. Each Sunday, I look into all those faces. One is given new life by God through me in Baptism. Another is forgiven by God through me in Reconciliation. They are all loved by God through me. A troubled mother-

to-be guided by God through me. My words can impact life or death decisions! This reality can sometimes seem surreal, but the glory remains, whether I am in the moment or not. May we all be blessed with mindfulness and a thankful nature. May these pages, in full or in part, provide a springboard to captivate your flock! May God bless you as a guiding light to all. Item C8 - $10

Trust and Transform, Cycle C - I would like to reflect on another theme that is central to today's gospel: the idea of "change." Jesus' life was all about change. He came to change the world, to teach us how to do a better job of loving God and loving one another... When Jesus called people to change their lives, it didn't always happen. We have a free will to accept what God has spoken to us or to reject it. Every other time Jesus told something to change, however, it always happened, whether he was changing a blind person into a person with sight, or a lame person into one who was ambulatory, or whether it was a storm on the sea that he told to calm down. Why do many people then not believe in the Eucharist? Because he said at the Last Supper as he handed the apostles bread: "this is my body," and likewise with the cup of wine: "this is my blood." We can believe that the bread and wine were truly changed when he said those sacred words. We just can't see it. I might add, we can't always believe what we see, but we can always believe what Jesus said. C9 - $10

The Soul Who Could, Cycle A - It begins with Jesus feeding a crowd of 5000 people with 5 barley loaves and two fish. None of the gospel stories tell us how he did it, but it must have been spectacular because it's the only miracle (other than the resurrection of Jesus himself) that all four gospels tell us about. The people were so impressed that they wanted to make Jesus their king. They didn't understand that he was already a king, but his kingdom was not of this world. He tried to explain that he didn't come to them to feed them free meals, but to feed them with a food that will bring them eternal life. "I am the bread that comes down from heaven, that a person eat it and never die." (Jn. 6,50) C10 - $10

Shepherds of Christ Ministries

(You may copy this page to order.)

Send Order To:
Shepherds of Christ Ministries
P.O. Box 627
Madison (China), Indiana 47250 USA

Order Form

	Qty	Total $
P1. Prayer Manuals ($0.50)	____	_____
P2. Spirituality Handbook ($3)	____	_____
BN1. Shepherds of Christ - Volume 1 ($15)	____	_____
BN2. Shepherds of Christ - Volume 2 ($15)	____	_____
BN3. Shepherds of Christ - Volume 3 ($10)	____	_____
BN4. Response to God's Love ($10)	____	_____
BN5. Response in Christ ($10)	____	_____
B7. Parents and Children's Rosary Book($10)	____	_____
B8. Mass Book ($12)	____	_____
C2. Focusing on the Word - Cycle B ($15)	____	_____
C3. Feed My Soul - Cycle C ($15)	____	_____
C4. Steadfast to the Son - Cycle A ($15)	____	_____
C5. Reflect on the Word - Cycle B ($15)	____	_____
C6. Centered in Christ - Cycle C ($10)	____	_____
C7. Inspired To Be Genuine - Cycle A ($10)	____	_____
C8. By God Through Me - Cycle B ($10)	____	_____
C9. Trust and Transform - Cycle C ($10)	____	_____
C10. The Soul Who Could - Cycle A ($10)	____	_____
Totals:	____	_____

Name: _____

Address: _____

City: _____ State: _____ Zip: _____

For More Information Call Toll free USA: 1-888-211-3041
or on the Internet: www.sofc.org

We pray for you from our Church in China,
24 hours a day before the exposed Eucharist.
We pray eight-day retreats for you every month.